The
EINSTEIN
SYNDROME

BY THE SAME AUTHOR

Economics: Analysis and Issues
Classical Economics Reconsidered
Knowledge and Decisions
Marxism: Philosophy and Economics
Say's Law
Basic Economics

The
EINSTEIN
SYNDROME

Bright Children Who Talk Late

ooooo

T H O M A S   S O W E L L

BASIC
BOOKS

A Member of the Perseus Books Group

Published by Basic Books,
A Member of the Perseus Books Group

Set in 11.5 Adobe Caslon by Perseus Publishing Services.

Cataloging-in-Publication data is available from the Library of Congress.
ISBN 978-0-465-08141-7

20 19 18 17

To Steven Pinker and Stephen Camarata
—friends in need and friends indeed.

CONTENTS

PREFACE

This book is about a very special set of children who have seldom been studied before—children who are exceptionally bright and also exceptionally slow to develop the ability to speak.

The first study of a group of such children was my book *Late-Talking Children*, published in 1997. That book was primarily about a group of 46 youngsters, whose parents formed a network across the country. This book is not primarily about that group, but incorporates new information from scientific studies, as well as new personal histories, and data from a subsequent study of a new group of 239 children like those in my group by Professor Stephen M. Camarata, a speech-language pathologist at the Vanderbilt University Medical Center. *The Einstein Syndrome* also draws upon many personal histories of people who were not part of either group.

While some people saw *Late-Talking Children* as simply anecdotal evidence about individuals, *The Einstein Syndrome* begins by focussing in the first chapter on hard statistical data about the highly unusual individual and family patterns found in both my group and Professor Camarata's group. Against that background, subsequent discussions of individual histories can be seen as confirmations and examples of those patterns, rather than as mere isolated anecdotes. Moreover, most of these histories are about different people than those covered in the first book.

Once the patterns have been established, both from statistics and from histories of flesh-and-blood people, the next step is to seek some explanations of these highly unusual patterns. That is attempted in Chapter 4 ("Groping for Answers"). Chapter 5 then goes into the painful dilemmas involved in evaluations of these children and Chapter 6 considers the pros and cons of putting a particular child in a particular early intervention program. Finally, Chapter 7 deals with what parents can do to cope with the uncertainties that remain, even after our best efforts to determine why this set of bright children talk late, and deals with the even more difficult question as to why a particular parent's particular child talks late. Some afterthoughts about the further implications of this study are expressed in the epilogue.

There are no easy answers or magic formulas. Yet there is enough solid information to enable parents to resist those who claim to have easy answers or magic formulas.

For many parents, the most serious problem with their late-talking child does not come from the speech delay, as such, but from the fears surrounding what that delay might mean for the future and from the reactions of other adults to that delay. Relatives, neighbors, teachers, day care center workers and others have often inflicted much needless anxiety and anguish on parents with thoughtless remarks and reckless attempts at diagnosis. Mothers are especially likely to be blamed for the child's speech delay, even when the same parents have raised other children who talked at the normal time or even earlier than normal. Perhaps worst of all, there are people who exploit parental fears to try to steer their children into programs that may not be right for the particular child.

There are so many wholly different reasons why children talk late that there can be no one-size-fits-all explanation or treatment. Deafness, mental retardation, autism, and physical problems with ears, tongue or palate are all possibilities. So is the special set of characteristics discussed in this book and called the Einstein syndrome, where none of these disabilities is present, but where the child follows a special development pattern found in a number of both famous and unknown people—including, of course, Albert Einstein.

No responsible parents are likely to simply *assume* that their particular late-talking child has the Einstein syndrome without having had physicians and others test for and rule out more dire possibilities. If anything, parents are more likely to continue to worry, even after repeated tests turn up nothing wrong, while the child shows every sign of being very bright and exhibits all the other characteristics discussed in this book.

In addition to their natural concerns and apprehensions, parents may be subjected to pressure from others to "do something." These may be relatives, friends, neighbors, or people promoting various programs in schools or elsewhere. But, if qualified medical and other highly-trained specialists say to let the child develop in his or her own way, then that may be the "something" that should be done.

For other children—perhaps most children who talk late—early intervention may be the way to go. Children with the characteristics discussed in this book are probably a minority among those who talk late.

Most parents of the kinds of children discussed here have never seen another child like their own. Letters that poured in to me after I first publicly discussed this subject often expressed a great sense of relief just to know that there was another child somewhere with the same set of characteristics as theirs. Yet such children are not quite as rare as they may seem. Over all, I have heard from the parents of well over a hundred such children.

Parents who know of no other child like their own may nevertheless know some adult who went through the same stages as a child. Such adults seldom talk about such things and many are themselves wholly unaware of having gone through such stages as small children. Two friends of mine discovered that they had been late-talkers only after they mentioned my study to their mothers. My college room mate knew that he had talked late, but I learned about it only years after we had both graduated. In short, while children with the characteristics described in this book are rare, they are not quite so rare as they might seem to their parents.

Thomas Sowell
Hoover Institution
Stanford University

ACKNOWLEDGEMENTS

This study would have been impossible without the cooperation of many parents, who filled out long questionnaires and wrote numerous letters describing their experiences and the experiences of their late-talking children. Professor Stephen M. Camarata of Vanderbilt University has been enormously helpful, not only to me but also to many parents who wrote to him for advice, for referrals, or to join his support group of parents of children with speech delays. His generosity in making his statistical data available to me has been an invaluable contribution to this book. An even more important role, in the long run, is his on-going research on bright children who talk late, drawing upon his own professional training in this area and both his clinical and personal experiences. As he follows these children into adulthood in the years to come, much more will become known, not only about these children but also about the validity or lack of validity of various evaluations that they have received. Since I am not of an age to expect to be able to follow the children in my group into adulthood, Professor Camarata has kindly agreed to include them in follow-up studies when I am no longer able to do so.

Among other professionals who have helped me in a variety of ways are noted language authority and neuroscientist Professor Steven Pinker of M.I.T., Professor Ellen Winner of Boston College, and Dr. Thelma E. Weeks, author of a 1974 book titled

The Slow Speech Development of a Bright Child. The generosity of all these people is hereby gratefully acknowledged. Needless to say, any errors or inadequacies of mine cannot be blamed on them. As with all my writings of the past dozen years, the work of my research assistant Na Liu has also been indispensable—particularly so in this case, where she has made computer program modifications to accommodate both Professor Camarata's data and mine.

Chapter 1

Patterns:
Family and Child

*Many, many parents of late talkers get advice on
how to fix things and many of them have a lot of
guilt. But I rarely encounter parents who are actually
in any way responsible for the late talking.*
— Professor Stephen Camarata
Vanderbilt University Medical Center

This book is about very bright children who are unusually late—
sometimes years behind schedule—in beginning to talk. Most
bright children are not late in talking and most children who are
late in talking are not exceptionally bright. But there is a special set
of youngsters with a distinctive set of characteristics—and whose
families also have a distinctive set of characteristics—whose speech
development lags far behind that of other children their age, while
their intellectual development surges ahead of that of their peers.
The most famous such person was Albert Einstein, but there have
been many others.

In a world where there are "norms" set for when infants are supposed to do everything—sit up, crawl, walk, talk—many parents

nervously compare when their own child does these things with when they are supposed to do them, according to the charts, books, and magazines. Where these parents are in contact with other parents whose children are the same age, their anxieties may be magnified if little Johnny is not doing things as early as a neighbor's little Susie.

In the end, nearly all people walk, talk, learn to use the bathroom, and read and write. In later life, no one is ever likely to know or care when they first did any of these things. But, of course, parents of small children are rightly focused very anxiously on the present as a young life unfolds before their eyes. No doubt norms can be useful to parents, physicians, and others who deal with small children, and who must be on the lookout for problems and dangers. In some cases, however, these norms may do more harm than good. Norms are based on averages and there is often much variation around those averages.

Norms can hang like a dark cloud over those parents whose children pass their second, third, or even fourth birthday without speaking. Tragic as this may be when the child is retarded or deaf, parents eventually come to terms with this. But those parents who are most likely to be continually torn with contradictory feelings and to hear conflicting conclusions from others, including experts, are those whose children show every sign of being bright—often strikingly brighter in some ways than other children their age—and yet who remain silent, while the children of neighbors and friends develop the ability to speak at the normal time.

I am the father of such a child and, four years ago, I published the first study of such children. (My son, incidentally, is today a computer software engineer).

There were many studies of late-talking children in general before mine—but none focussing on *very bright* children who are years behind schedule in speaking. While it was known that Einstein was such a child, there was little or no awareness of how many other very bright people were also years late in talking. Indeed, I was continually surprised to discover how many such people there were, in all walks of life, famous and unknown.

Many parents who read my book *Late-Talking Children* wrote to me to say that they were astonished to read about things that seemed like an eye-witness description of their own child and their own family. One mother said that she got goose bumps reading descriptions that fit her child and her family so closely, while other mothers have reported simply weeping as they read for the first time something that so obviously fitted their own puzzling child. The number of such children whose parents wrote to me after the book was published far exceeded the 46 children covered in that book.

Now, four years later, it is possible not only to follow the progress of that original set of children, but also to draw upon new research on an even larger sample of other bright children who talked late by Professor Stephen Camarata of the Vanderbilt University medical school. In addition to being a psychologist specializing in childhood language disorders and the author of articles on the subject, Professor Camarata is also the father of a late-talking child and he himself was three and a half years old before he began to speak.

Before setting forth the patterns found in both our studies and the further development of the children in the original group that was studied, it is necessary to warn parents that not all children who talk late are like the children in these studies. False hope can be as cruel as unnecessary despair. Children can talk late for a wide variety of reasons. Some have physical defects in their ears or their tongues or elsewhere. Some are autistic. Their mental levels range from severely retarded on up to the level of late-talkers who have grown up and gone on to win Nobel Prizes in economics and in physics.

Many studies of late-talking children compare this entire highly heterogenous group with "normal" children and find that, on average, late-talkers are usually somewhat behind in intellectual skills and often have other lasting problems. Yet, when these studies break down this very disparate group into (1) those who neither speak nor understand what is said to them and (2) those who clearly understand but just do not talk, the latter typically do much better and are more likely to develop normally.[1] My study and that of Professor Camarata are the first to focus more narrowly on late-talking children who are not merely normal in intelligence but above normal. Although there were no studies of such children just five years ago, now there are two and the two groups of children and their families can be compared.

What do we now know about such children and their families?

FAMILY PATTERNS

The families in both studies of bright children who talk late are very atypical. The great majority of these children have close relatives in highly analytical occupations, such as engineers, scientists, and mathematicians. The typical child in these two samples also has multiple close relatives who play a musical instrument, some as professional musicians. This is not just a matter of an engineer here or a musician there. Usually the same child has a number of close relatives in these categories. The median number in my study was four and the range was from one child with none to three children with nine such close relatives each.

This is all the more remarkable because the term "close relatives" was used very narrowly in my study to include only parents, grandparents, uncles and aunts. It did not include even first cousins. Professor Camarata's study used a similarly restricted definition of close relatives, except that his study included siblings, which my study neglected to do.

The general patterns found among the 43 biological families in my study were quite similar to those found in the 232 biological families who joined Professor Camarata's group during its first two years. My group was originally formed for mutual support, rather than research, and had grown to 55 families by the time I sent out the survey whose results were presented in *Late-Talking Children*. Of these 55 families, 44 filled out the questionnaires that I sent them and these 44 families contained 46 late-talking children, since two families had two late-talkers each. Because one child was adopted and his biological family was unknown, there were 43 biological families in my study. In Professor Camarata's study, there were 235 families, of whom 232 were biological families, since two families had adopted a child who talked late and one family had such a child born as a result of being fathered by an unknown sperm donor. Altogether, there were 239 children in his group at the end of two years, of whom 236 were biological children of their respective families.

Professor Camarata's group was not only much larger, but also grew faster and continued growing after membership in my group was closed. In June 2000, he was generous enough to provide me with data on the families who had joined during the first two years of his research. This allows the patterns found in the two studies to be compared, as regards both individuals and families.

Analytical Occupations

The most striking thing about the families in both groups are their highly atypical—and highly analytical—occupations. Seventy-four percent of the biological children in my study and 70 percent of the biological children in the study conducted by Professor Camarata had at least one close relative who was either an engineer, a scientist or a mathematician. Engineers alone were close relatives of 60 percent of the children in my group and 59 percent of the children in Camarata's group.

Other occupations requiring highly analytical education were also heavily represented among the close relatives of the children in both groups. The table below shows the respective percentages of the biological children who had close relatives in the following occupations:

	ORIGINAL STUDY	CAMARATA STUDY
Accountants	53 percent	38 percent
Computer Specialists	35 percent	44 percent
Engineers	60 percent	59 percent
Mathematicians	5 percent	17 percent
Physicians	12 percent	19 percent
Pilots	14 percent	13 percent
Scientists	20 percent	18 percent
Other Analytical Occupations	5 percent *	20 percent
AT LEAST ONE OF THE ABOVE	**86 percent**	**89 percent**
TWO OR MORE OF THE ABOVE	**65 percent**	**70 percent**

* two economists

How unusual are these families? Ideally, we would like to compare them with families of the same size, age and socioeconomic circumstances in the general population. But that is neither feasible nor necessary. We know that three-fifths of the children in the general population cannot have engineers as close relatives, simply because there are not nearly enough engineers in the country for that to be true. Similarly with people in other analytical occupations. These are highly unusual families that the late-talking children in both our groups come from. When all the close relatives in highly analytical occupations are counted, the families in both these groups are clearly skewed in the direction of unusual mathematical and other analytical abilities.

Such a high incidence of close family members in highly analytical occupations is unusual, not only as compared to the population at large, but also as compared to late-talking children in general. A study in England of late-talking children in general found that only two percent of the fathers of these British children with language delays were engineers.[2] By contrast, 20 percent of the children in my group and 22 percent of the children in Camarata's group have fathers who are engineers. Children with the Einstein syndrome are not just late-talkers. They and their families have a whole set of other atypical characteristics, as will become clearer as the data are examined.

Such high concentrations of engineers in these families would be remarkable enough if engineering were the only highly analytical occupation among the relatives of these children. But, when other professions such as mathematician, scientist, computer specialist, pilot, economist, and accountants are added, then 37 of the 43 biological families in my group have at least one close relative of the child in such fields and most have more than one.[3] The same general pattern was found in Stephen Camarata's group, where 210 out of 232 biological families have at least one close relative of the child in these analytical occupations.

Music

Three quarters of the biological children in my group had at least one close relative who played a musical instrument. That includes 57 percent who had *multiple* musicians among their close relatives. Among parents alone, at least one parent played a musical instrument in just over half of the families. Professional musicians were close relatives of 26 percent of the biological children in my group.

In Camarata's group, 78 percent of the biological children had at least one close relative who played a musical instrument and 66 percent had multiple musicians among close relatives. Twenty-eight percent of the biological children in his group had a professional musician among their close relatives. Again, these are highly unusual proportions of people who play musical instruments, especially at the professional level, and lends further support to the picture of people with unusual—and probably hereditary—kinds of specialized abilities.

When analytical and musical occupations are considered together, only 3 of the 43 biological families in my group failed to have a close relative of the late-talking child in one of these fields. Most had multiple members in such fields. In Camarata's group, only 4 percent of the families (12 out of 232) were without a close relative of the child in any of these analytical occupations and without a close relative who played a musical instrument. That is not very different from the 7 percent in my study. More than nine out of ten of the biological children in his group (91 percent) had two or more close relatives in either of these categories and more than four out of five (83 percent) had three or more close relatives in these categories.

Educational Levels

The parents of the children in both groups are above average in education. Nearly three out of five (59 percent) of the parents in my group had completed at least four years of college, including 27 percent who had postgraduate education. In Camarata's group, 71 percent of the parents had four years of college, including 26 percent who had postgraduate education.

Since many financial and social conditions are involved in getting a higher education, this is not as strong evidence of unusual hereditary mental abilities as the data on analytical occupations and musicians. However, it is consistent with the other indications of atypical families.

Late-Talking Relatives

Were there other late-talkers among the close relatives of the children studied? In my group, 26 percent of the children had a close relative who talked late and in Camarata's group 48 percent of the children had a close relative who talked late. However, the majority of parents in both groups—and among many others outside these groups whom I have heard from—have no other child like their own among their close relatives.

Many parents said that they had never seen or heard of a child like theirs. That has contributed to a great sense of utter isolation and bafflement often expressed by parents of very bright children who talk late. Those parents who did report having another late-talker among their relatives, especially when these other late talkers had turned out fine, often reported that this gave them hope, even when "experts" made dire predictions about their children.

PATTERNS AMONG THE CHILDREN

What patterns did we find among the children themselves? The children in both studies differ from children in general in sex ratios, ability patterns, and social characteristics. Since we are now considering individuals, rather than families, here we count all the children—46 in my group and 239 in Professor Camarata's group—regardless of whether they are or are not the biological children.

Sex Ratios

The overwhelming majority of the late-talking children in my group and in Professor Camarata's group are boys. Eighty-seven percent of the children in my original group of 55 late-talking children, which began forming in 1993, were boys. Among the 46 children surveyed, 89 percent were boys. In Professor Camarata's group of 236 biological children, 85 percent were boys, with the same percentage being boys among the total of 239 children in his sample. Yet those relatively few late-talkers in our groups who are girls share the same individual and family patterns as the boys. For example, five of the seven girls in my group had at least one engineer as a close relative and five of the seven also had at least one close relative who played a musical instrument. All of these were biological children. In Camarata's group, 24 of the 36 girls who were biological children had an engineer as a close relative and 31 of these 36 girls had at least one close relative who played a musical instrument.

In terms of their own behavior, the girls in both groups are so similar to boys that—with one exception—their data are not listed separately here. For example, 75 percent of the girls and 77 percent of the boys in Professor Camarata's group like building things. (This question was not covered in my survey.)

Mental Abilities

The children in both studies show the same skew in the direction of highly analytical abilities that their relatives show. While still toddlers, most excel in putting puzzles together, sometimes including puzzles designed for older children or adults. Poetry, art or social skills seldom figure prominently among their interests or achievements, either as children or adults.

Surprisingly few of the children in either study had been given formal intelligence tests—despite their delay in speech development. Perhaps this was because the parents had seen enough signs of their precocious mental abilities to have no serious doubts on that score. Indeed, it was often the contrast between their intellectual progress and their delayed speech that proved so baffling to parents and professionals alike.

In both studies, parents were asked to rate their children's abilities in solving puzzles as average, below average or unusually good. Here are the breakdowns for both groups:

	ORIGINAL STUDY	CAMARATA STUDY
Unusually Good	67 percent	46 percent
Average	15 percent	37 percent
Below Average	11 percent	8 percent
Not Noticed	7 percent	7 percent

While the children in Camarata's group were not as heavily concentrated in the top category, that was still the category with the most children, and just 8 percent were rated "below average" on puzzles, compared to 11 percent in my group. Nor can these ratings be dismissed as optimistic parental bias, for only a minority of these same parents rated their children above average on physical skills—35 percent in my study and 37 percent in Camarata's study—and in both groups an absolute majority of the parents rated their children below average or far below average in social development.

Memory is another aspect of mental ability. Here again, the most common rating in both studies was the highest rating:

	ORIGINAL STUDY	CAMARATA STUDY
Extremely Good	59 percent	52 percent
Above Average	42 percent	33 percent
Average	none	13 percent
Below Average	none	1 percent
Very Poor	none	7 percent

In short, both studies find parental ratings of these children's memories heavily skewed toward the upper extreme. In my study, many parents wrote in such comments as "truly unbelievable" or, in one case, simply an exclamation point. Many of these parents, as well as many other parents that I have heard from who were not part of my group, have given vivid examples of their children's extraordinary memories or have characterized these memories as "photographic."

Perhaps not surprisingly, among the children's likes and dislikes, puzzles figured prominently. In Professor Camarata's study, puzzles were included among the child's likes in 82 percent of the cases where the parents answered and among their dislikes in only 4 percent of these cases. Eighty-six percent liked computers and 97 percent liked music. Only one of the 239 children disliked music and none disliked computers.

Here my survey was somewhat different and less focussed, in that I simply asked parents to list their child's likes and dislikes, without providing any specific choices, while Camarata's survey listed choices and boxes to check for both likes and dislikes. By and large, my percentages for the things children liked were much lower on all these things, though computers, music and puzzles were the top three choices in my study as well.

Incidentally, the high proportion of the children who liked computers is particularly striking because many of the children were pre-schoolers or toddlers when their families were surveyed. Late-talking children as young as two years of age have been reported as being able to use computers without adult help. Indeed, one of the five-year-old pre-schoolers in my group helped both his mother at home and his teacher at school when they had problems using the computer. He could also play the piano with his eyes closed.

Social Characteristics

Social development is a problem area for most of the children in both studies. In addition to being late in talking, most of them are also late in socializing with their peers and late in toilet training.

In terms of their interactions with other people, most of the children in both groups were rated below average:

	ORIGINAL STUDY	**CAMARATA STUDY**
Far Above Average	2 percent	3 percent
Above Average	15 percent	11 percent
Average	13 percent	29 percent
Below Average	43 percent	47 percent
Far Below Average	26 percent	9 percent

In short, more than two thirds of the children in my study were rated either below average or far below average, as were more than half of the children in Camarata's study. Many parents are understandably worried that their unusual children will grow up to be anti-social adults or that they will suffer as a result of their anti-social behavior in childhood. However, these ratings of social development were made while most of these late-talking children were still very young.

My survey also included six adults who had talked late. Four of them were rated either above average or far above average in social development. In so far as we can rely on such a small sample, it suggests that the social lag of late-talking children is not a sign of pre-destined anti-social behavior for life. Camarata's survey did not include this question. However, my own observations of adults who had talked late, including Professor Camarata himself, suggest no such anti-social patterns. On more than one occasion, Camarata has been the life of the party. However, some late-talkers do remain shy or anti-social, just as some people do who begin speaking at the usual time.

Another aspect of social development is meeting new people. Camarata's survey asked whether the children liked meeting new people, but mine did not. Here the results are quite mixed and, since this is one of the few areas where boys and girls differ somewhat, they are listed separately.

Meeting New People	Boys	Girls
Likes very much	16 percent	19 percent
Likes somewhat	30 percent	38 percent
Neutral or unknown	26 percent	22 percent
Dislikes somewhat	24 percent	11 percent
Dislikes very much	3 percent	4 percent
No data	1 percent	0 percent

While a slight majority of the girls and a near majority of the boys like meeting new people, there is a noticeable difference between the sexes in the proportion who actually dislike meeting new people—27 percent of the boys versus 15 percent of the girls.

Another problem area for children in both groups has been toilet training. Most children in the general population become toilet trained when they are between two and three years old. In neither of the groups of late-talking children studied was the average age of toilet training that early. In my group, the median age for toilet training was the same for both urination and bowel movements—between three and three-and-a-half years old. In Professor

Camarata's group, the median age of toilet training for urination was likewise between three and three and a half—for those who had achieved toilet training, about half of the children in his group. For bowel movement, the median age of toilet training in his group was between three and a half and four for that half who had in fact become toilet trained at the time of the survey.

The average age of the children in Camarata's group is younger than the average age of the children in my group[4] which may be why more of the children in his group have not yet become toilet trained. There were also wide variations in both groups, with some of the children being toilet trained before their second birthday, while a few of the children in both groups were five years old before becoming toilet trained.

One of the phrases that appears again and again in communications from parents of these late-talking children is "strong-willed." These include not only parents of the children in these two studies but also many other parents who have contacted Professor Camarata or me without joining either group. The same pattern of early independence, marching to their own drummer, or just plain stubbornness, can also be seen in the biographies of famous people who talked late, as will become apparent in the next chapter. However, this is not something on which either study collected data. It was just a comment that many parents volunteered in both groups and among those who contacted us without joining either group.

Some of the patterns found among both groups of late-talking children overlap with patterns found in two other kinds of children—high-IQ children in general and autistic children. A study of high-IQ children by Professor Ellen Winner of Boston College found a set of social characteristics that will be familiar to many parents of late-talking children like those in my group and in Stephen Camarata's group. These are also characteristics that can get children labelled "autistic" by evaluators who simply go down a checklist of symptoms.

The obsessive interests, abnormal sensitivities, extreme reactions, and prodigious memories that Professor Winner found among high-IQ children have also been found among autistic children. But that is wholly different from saying that we can infer autism whenever such characteristics are present—even when they are present in children who are behind schedule in beginning to speak. Yet that is the inference that is too often made by evaluators who mechanically go down a checklist of symptoms.

Quote	Page
They develop almost obsessive interests in specific areas, such as computers...	29
These children have been reported to show intense reactions to noise, pain, and frustration.	27
They refuse to submit to any task that does not engage them and, as a result, often end up labeled as hyperactive or with an attention deficit disorder.	218
Gifted children in all areas seem to march to their own drummer.	218
They often play alone and enjoy solitude, not only because they like to but also because they have few people to play with that have the same interests.	30
They have predigious memories...	29

SOURCE: Ellen Winner *Gifted Children: Myths and Realities* (New York: Basic Books, 1996)

Before such terms as "hyperactive," "attention deficit disorder," or "autism" were coined, such children were often considered to be simply mentally retarded. These include physicists Edward Teller and Albert Einstein, as well as famed nineteenth-century pianist Clara Schumann, all of whom were thought to be mentally subnormal when they were small children.

Professor Winner's study was not the first to note the highly selective interests of very bright children. The famous Terman study at Stanford University, which followed high-IQ children through-out their lifetimes, found them likewise highly selective in what they took an interest in and in what they did well.[5]

The very independent and selective interests of bright children not only present a problem when they are being evaluated because of speech delays, these same characteristics can present continuing problems in schools or classes that neglect intellectual substance for "activities" or "projects" that teachers may find "exciting" but which children with analytical minds find boring. These inadequacies of the school work can all too easily be projected as inadequacies of the child, who may be labeled as having "attention deficit hyperactivity disorder" instead of as simply being bored by what the school offers. Ritalin has too often been used as a substitute for intellectually challenging education.

DEVELOPMENT PATTERNS

When did these children begin to talk? It depends on whether speaking isolated words is considered to be talking or whether that term is reserved for multi-word statements, complete sentences or back-and-forth conversation.

Most of the children in my group had spoken at least a word before they were two and a half years old. In Stephen Camarata's group, most had spoken at least a word by the time them were one and a half. But most parents do not consider saying an isolated word to be talking, especially since some late-talking children say isolated words very infrequently and can go months or even years before adding anything more to their vocabulary. Moreover, a word may be no more than a sound that a child likes to make, unless it is used to identify some person, thing, or feeling.

Most of the children in my group did not make a statement using more than one word until they were at least three and a half years old and their first complete sentence was spoken when they were four. Here it is difficult to make comparisons with the children in Stephen Camarata's group, who were almost certainly younger than the children in my group as of the time of the respective surveys.[6] In both groups there were children who were not yet speaking words or sentences, much less engaging in back-and-forth conversation. But these were a minority of the children in my group and were more than half of the children in Professor Camarata's group when it came to complete sentences and back-and-forth conversation. Among those children in his group who were in fact making multi-word statements, the first such statement came by age three and a half for most of the children and the first complete sentence not before age five.

It was not until age four that most of the children in my group were able to have back-and-forth conversation. For the children in Camarata's group, it was not before age six—and 58 percent had not yet reached the point of talking back and forth. Again, it is necessary to emphasize that the children in Camarata's group tend to be younger than the children in my group.

In both groups, there were great variations among the children. Two of the children in my group did not even speak their first word until they were three and a half years old, and one of the children in Camarata's group did not speak that first word until age four. Meanwhile, there were children in both groups who spoke their first word before they were a year old.

In short, there is no standard way in which late-talking children like these finally begin to speak. It may be slowly or suddenly and their speech may be clearly articulate or incomprehensible at first. Some begin to speak as other children do, first in babbles and isolated words, and then proceed in stages toward normal speech, only later than other children. In other cases, however, children with delayed speech development did not coo or babble as other infants do, but remained silent right up to the moment when they suddenly startled their parents by speaking a complete sentence.

Even after a child has begun to speak, the development of speech may proceed very unevenly. A late-talking little girl who was studied closely back in 1925 had only a five-word vocabulary when she was 24 months old, and this rose gradually to 123 words when she was 39 months old. (This was fewer words than her sister had at half that age.) Then her vocabulary nearly doubled to 240 words in her 40th month and more than doubled again to 490 words in her 41st month. In period of a year and a half, her vocabulary had grown nearly one hundred-fold, while becoming more sophisticated as well.[7]

Even after late-talking children begin to speak, the quantity of talk may vary enormously from child to child, some unleashing a flood of words and others remaining silent for months after first speaking. A professor at the University of Michigan told of his silent, three-year-old son's response to an incident involving his older brother:

> The older boy, now five, had learned to read and would entertain his doting parents by doing so aloud. One evening he came upon a word he did not recognize, and struggled with it. At which point his brother toddled over, peered at the text and read out the sentence perfectly. Following that, he again lapsed into silence for several months and only then began to speak easily.[8]

Just as norms for when children talk cannot be taken as rigid, neither can norms for the manner in which their speech will develop. Even after they begin to speak, some of these children say very little, while others have become so talkative that some parents have said: "Now I wish he would shut up!" Other late-talkers have remained taciturn even as adults—as, of course, do some other people who began speaking at the normal time.

When some of these children begin to talk, and for some time thereafter, what they say may be virtually incomprehensible to most people, though some family members may develop an ability to figure out what they mean. Other late-talkers are clear as a bell from the moment when they finally begin to speak. In short, not only do the children studied not conform to general norms in their speech development, there are few norms of their own. They march to their own drummers in this, as in other things.

Speech therapy seems to help some children to talk but others remain impervious to all efforts, parental or professional. Both with speech and with toilet training, a parent who has tried everything with no success, and has finally just given up, may later be surprised to find the child suddenly doing on his own what others have long attempted in vain to get him to do.

NUMBERS

How many children are there like these in the general population—that is, precociously analytical children who are late in beginning to speak?

No one knows, and they are no doubt exceptions rather than the rule, even among children who talk late. But still I have been amazed at how many I have learned about informally, without looking for them, just as a result of mentioning the subject, mentioning my study or mentioning the book that resulted from it. Sometimes I have discovered that people I already knew fit this pattern, though I had not known that they talked late until I brought up the subject.

The first person I knew who talked late, besides my son, was my college room-mate. But I never knew that he had talked late when we were in college together. Only years later, when the subject came up in connection with my son and my study did his story come out.

My ex-room mate is now a professor of mathematics at a well-known college. Late-talking children often go on to excel in mastering logic-based systems—whether mathematics, chess, computers, or pianos.

Another person whom I knew for decades before learning that he talked late was my friend and fellow economist, Walter Williams. Indeed, Walter himself did not know that he had talked late until he mentioned my study to his mother and she informed him. Another friend who has helped me with my computer problems likewise did not know that he had talked late until he mentioned my study to his mother. When he told her about the unusual children I had discovered, she said: "Like you!"

When I completed the manuscript of *Late-Talking Children* in 1996, two publishers expressed interest in it. The assistant to one of these publishers revealed that he had talked late. The head of the other publishing house had also talked late—and had been a professional musician before going into publishing.

While spending a week in New Zealand in 1996, I happened to mention my study at two gatherings there and learned of someone like the children in my study on each occasion. Both late-talkers were now grown. One is an engineer and the other a mathematician.

In the spring of 1997, I learned of four more such people—again, just incidentally when my study was mentioned. One was a professor of mathematics at Wabash College, where I was giving a talk on an unrelated topic. When my wife mentioned at work that she was going to take a week off to accompany me on a book tour, her co-workers of course wanted to know what the book was about. After she told them, they brought forth three more examples of such children that they knew about. One young man was currently in medical school. Another was an undergraduate at the University of California at Davis, where he was on the dean's list, and he also played in a local symphony orchestra. The third late-talker that my wife learned about was still in elementary school, where he was already regarded as a math and computer whiz.

My first formal presentation on this subject was at the Harvard Club of New York, where I gave a talk in August, 1997. The audience included several parents of bright children who had talked late, some of whom were now grown. Most of these children came from families similar to those in the group I had studied, and these children had personal characteristics similar to those of the children in our group. I continued to encounter examples of such children, whether on talk shows, by mail, by phone, or when giving speeches.

One of my earliest media interviews was by telephone with a radio program called "Education Tuesday," broadcast on National Public Radio from Wisconsin. During the hour that I was on the air, five people phoned in about bright children who talked late— and all five children had an engineer as a close relative, much to the astonishment of the hostess of the program. Similar stories later came in from listeners to other talk shows on which I was interviewed. Two of the talk show hosts themselves—Barry Farber and G. Gordon Liddy—revealed that they had talked late.

It was as a result of hearing me on another radio broadcast on National Public Radio, the "Diane Rehm Show" from Washington, D.C., that Professor Stephen Camarata of Vanderbilt University contacted me and offered to be of help in any way that he could. It was a generous offer on his part and it was a great relief to me to be able to refer parents of late-talking children to someone with a Ph.D. in speech pathology and experience in running his own clinic for such children. Professor Camarata then began to form his own group of parents of late-talking children and do research on them. He has also formed a foundation to support research that will follow these children into adulthood.

After returning home from my book tour, I found a message on my telephone answering machine from Congressman Dick Armey, who said that he had talked late. He too was in an analytical occupation—a professor of economics—before going into politics. I also learned independently that one of Congressman Armey's legislative aides had a brother who talked late—and who scored a perfect 800 on the mathematics portion of the Scholastic Aptitude Test.

A professor at a prestigious university wrote to me about his grandson who was late in talking. The family contained a very large number of scientists and musicians. However, the little boy's parents were so sensitive about his delayed speech development that this professor confessed that he dared not bring up the subject, even to tell them about my book. Later, they discovered the book themselves and told him about it, so that now he was free to talk with them on the subject.

I also learned that a distant relative of mine and his wife had the same sensitivity about their late-talking child, so I sent a copy of my book to a family member who was closer to them and who would know how to broach the subject diplomatically.

As my files on late-talking children grew, I decided to order two more filing cabinets to hold it all. One of the two young men who delivered the filing cabinets to my home turned out to have a little sister who had talked late and who was now in school, where she was an outstanding student.

Two years later, on October 5, 1999, I happened to learn of two late-talkers on the same day. In the morning, while meeting with the editorial staff of the *Orange County Register* in Santa Ana, California, I mentioned *Late-Talking Children* and one of the editors said that his brother had talked late. When I asked what his brother was doing now, the editor replied that he had gotten a Ph.D. in mathematics. That evening, at a Los Angeles gathering sponsored by the Hoover Institution, Nobel Prizewinning economist Gary Becker revealed that he was two and a half years old before he began to speak.

After a television broadcast about late-talking children on "Dateline.NBC" on March 17, 1999, hundreds of e-mails, letters and phone calls were received by Camarata—and quite a few by me. One sign of how much the word was spreading was that it took three years for 55 families to join my original group of parents of late-talking children, but Camarata's group surpassed that in just one year and had more than 200 families a year after that. While my group is scattered across the United States, Camarata's group also includes members in Brazil, New Zealand, Malaysia and Dubai as well, and he has also received inquiries about late-talking children from people in England, France, Italy, Spain, Cuba, Japan, Turkey, Romania, Slovenia and Saudi Arabia. The word about these highly unusual children has begun to spread abroad, though it has by no means spread fully within the United States.

PARENTAL CONCERNS

What worried most parents of the late-talking children in the groups surveyed by Stephen Camarata and myself? When did they first become worried?

More than half the parents in my group and in Professor Camarata's group had become seriously concerned about their child's lag in speech development by the time the child was two and a half years old. In both cases, the main reason for that concern was not that there were daily problems at the time, but that the child was so much behind schedule in beginning to speak. In some cases, the child's own frustrations at being unable to make himself understood were a consideration, but the fact that the child was behind schedule was a factor mentioned several times as often in both studies. These primary reasons for parental concern are shown in the following table:

	ORIGINAL STUDY	CAMARATA STUDY
Child's Frustration	9 percent	11 percent
Daily Problems	2 percent	9 percent
Behind Schedule	67 percent	65 percent
Other	22 percent	14 percent

From the time when the parents first became seriously concerned—and, for many parents, that meant real stress and even tears—to the time when the child finally began to talk was about two years on average for the parents in my group and three years for the parents in Professor Camarata's group. In both cases, that is a very long time to be under this kind of pressure, often aggravated by nagging doubts as to whether some deficiency in parenting might have been responsible for the child's speech delay. All too often, thoughtless comments by relatives and friends, as well as dire warnings based on hasty labels put on these children by professionals and semi-professionals, especially in schools, have added to the parents' anxieties and forebodings.

There are very real reasons to be concerned when a child is late in beginning to speak. Complacency would be dangerous. Fortunately, it would also be unlikely among parents with any sense of responsibility. What such parents need is both general information and specific—and multiple—professional evaluations of their own child. Obviously, this book can provide only the first. But that may turn out to be useful in choosing when, where and how to get evaluations of a particular child.

IMPLICATIONS

While the two studies that have been done on bright children who talk late have turned up striking statistical patterns that are remarkably similar to one another, the full story requires the personal experiences of these children and their families. These experiences can also tell us something about the many pitfalls that parents encounter in child care facilities and public schools, as well as in dealing with people in what are called "the helping professions"—but which are not always helpful and are sometimes harmful.

Some of these professionals do a wonderful job—that was certainly so with the speech therapist who helped my son learn to talk—but there are others, in this and other professions, who are not merely ineffective but counterproductive and destructive in many ways. The behavior of the children, the anxieties of the parents, and the influence of relatives, teachers, doctors, and others flesh out a picture whose skeletal patterns we have already seen in statistics.

The next two chapters explore these personal experiences. Then we begin in Chapter 4 to consider some possible general explanations for the anomaly that many brighter-than-average children began talking much later than their peers. In Chapter 5 we take a hard look at the evaluation process and, in Chapter 6, at the wide variety of things included in the omnibus category "early intervention." Finally, in Chapter 7, we confront the unavoidable question that each parent of a late-talking child must face: What can I do about it? There is no definitive answer to that question, but there are serious pitfalls in doing either too much or too little, and it is worth understanding what those pitfalls are.

What most parents are most concerned about are not the current problems associated with a child's delayed development of speech, but what that delayed speech portends for the years ahead, when the child becomes an adult. The next chapter will look at late-talking children who have grown up to become adults, including some very prominent adults.

In these stories, as well as in the stories of late-talkers who are still children, a recurrent theme will be what a professor at U.C.L.A.'s

Neuropsychiatric Institute once described as "the three M's—mathematics, music, and memory." A secondary theme will be these children's intense reactions to irritations and frustrations—a number of parents have reported world-class tantrums—similar to what Ellen Winner found among the high-IQ children that she studied.

Chapter 2

Adults Who Talked Late

Parents of children who are late in talking are ultimately concerned about how their children will turn out as adults. Will these children, for example, continue to show the shyness and social maladroitness that many have as children or is that something that will fade away over the years, as they acquire fluent speech and are therefore able to participate more easily in social activities? For many parents, the question is even more basic: Will their children be able to take care of themselves independently when they are grown?

There are enough late-talking children who grew up to become political figures or media figures to dispel the notion that shyness must be permanent. Benito Mussolini was certainly not shy. Nor are talk-show hosts G. Gordon Liddy and Barry Farber, economist-journalist Walter Williams, or House Majority Leader Dick Armey. Yet all of them were late in beginning to speak.

Even in fields not requiring much social interaction or social skills, such as science and engineering, late-talkers are not necessarily shy or withdrawn as adults. Nuclear physicist Richard Feynman was a late talker—and an extrovert. Although later destined to win a Nobel Prize, Feynman was just an unknown young scientist when he worked on the Manhattan Project that produced the first atomic bomb in Los Alamos, New Mexico. Yet the already legendary physicist Niels Bohr noticed that Feynman was one of the few people there who would dare to challenge his ideas. Bohr said to his son: "Remember the name of that little fellow in the back over there? He's the only guy who's not afraid of me, and will say when I've got a crazy idea. So *next* time when we want to discuss ideas, we're not going to be able to do it with these guys who say everything is yes, yes, Dr. Bohr. Get that guy and I'll talk to him first."[1]

Feynman also picked locks at Los Alamos and even purloined papers out of Edward Teller's desk, in order to demonstrate the inadequacies of the security system.[2] Introverted he was not. Many years later, Professor Feynman was described as "charismatic" in his appearances on television[3] and a student of his at Cal Tech described his lectures there in much the same way.[4]

There are other adults whose names have not been in the public eye who were late in talking, and yet who are in occupations requiring much social interaction. Among those that I know, one has run a day care center for senior citizens, which involves interacting not only with patients and staff, but also with members of his board of directors and with outside suppliers of the various goods and services needed to run the center. Professor Camarata of Vanderbilt is constantly interacting with children and parents, as well as with his students and colleagues in his professional work. In social settings, any parent who could see his infectious enthusiasm would be unburdened of the fear that late talking among children makes shyness or anti-social attitudes inevitable for them in adulthood.

Some late-talkers do, of course, tend to remain shy and socially maladroit as adults, but that is also true of many people who begin speaking at the normal time. How any given child's personality will turn out as an adult is as difficult to predict for late-talking children as for anyone else. But the early shyness and social awkwardness that is so often found among young late-talkers is not a sign of pre-destination. As for being able to take care of themselves as adults, financially and otherwise, that question has been answered in the affirmative by both famous and unknown adults who were late in talking as children.

PUBLIC FIGURES

The most famous late-talker was of course Albert Einstein, which is why the set of characteristics found among the children in our study is called "the Einstein syndrome." However, other famous physicists who also talked late include Edward Teller, later to become known as "the father of the H-Bomb," and the already mentioned Nobel Prize-winning physicist Richard Feynman of Cal Tech. All three played roles in the creation of the first atomic bomb.[5]

Feynman was two years old before he began to talk. According to his biographer, Feyman's mother "worried for months" and then suddenly he became "unstoppably voluble."[6] Einstein said that he was three years old when he began to talk, but some other members of his family said that he was two.[7] Whether the discrepancy was due to a difference in memories or different definitions of talking, he was still late. According to Edward Teller's biographer, at age three "he had yet to utter his first coherent word" and was "almost smug in his refusal to talk" when his grandfather "tried desperately" to get him to say something. Afterwards, his grandfather told young Teller's parents: "I think you should face the possibility that you have a retarded child."[8]

In the case of Einstein, even after he began to speak, his first teachers in elementary school "revived early fears that he was mentally retarded." He "ignored whatever bored him, making no attempt to master it; but if something caught his interest, he embraced it with the purposeful concentration of a watchmaker."[9] When his worried father asked the headmaster of the school his son attended what kind of occupation he should try to prepare the boy for, the reply was: "It doesn't matter; he'll never make a success of anything."[10]

Although the term "the Einstein syndrome" was coined simply to describe very bright children who are also very late in talking, in fact it turns out that the parallels go deeper. Einstein's father and an uncle were engineers. His mother played the piano and Einstein himself played the violin, beginning at age five and continuing throughout his mature years. He described music as "an inner necessity."[11]

Young Einstein's highly selective interests and unusual concentration on the things that attracted that interest were also common characteristics of the children studied here. So are early childhood temper tantrums. During one of these tantrums, he threw a stool at his tutor, who ran away and was never seen again.[12] Throwing things was something Einstein often did as a child when he was angry. On another occasion, he just missed his little sister with a bowling ball that he threw at her, and yet another time she was not quick enough to get out of the way when he hit her on the head with the handle of a garden hoe. In later life, however, he and his sister were very close. Einstein's tantrums stopped when he turned seven.[13]

As a young child, Einstein was "lonely and dreamy" and did not make friends easily. He preferred "solitary and taxing" pastimes, such as assembling complicated constructions with his building blocks and making houses of cards as much as fourteen stories high. Even after Einstein began to speak, he was neither fluent nor sure of himself. He "would softly repeat every sentence he uttered—a habit he continued until he was seven." He was still not yet fluent when he turned nine.[14]

While there may never be another Einstein, in terms of his analytical or creative genius, the thrust of the abilities of the children studied here have been in the same general analytical direction. Another possible parallel will be discussed in Chapter 4, when some explanations are sought for the unusual patterns found among these children and their families.

An uncle who had graduated from the Stuttgart Polytechnic Engineering School introduced Einstein to algebra and geometry. His private study of mathematics took him to integral calculus while his classmates were still studying decimals. But in subjects that did not interest him, he was so openly lackadaisical that one of his teachers suggested that he leave the school. Einstein himself later went to the principal of the gymnasium to ask for a letter certifying that he was ready to do university work in mathematics, even though he was not up to standard in other subjects such as history, geography or languages. Whether because of the principal's awareness of Einstein's prowess in mathematics or because he knew that the boy was a problem student whom the teachers would be glad to be rid of, he agreed to write the letter and Einstein was on a train within the hour.[15]

When young Edward Teller finally began to talk, as he turned four, "it was in sentences, not words."[16] Unusual as this might seem, some other late-talkers have done the same— Nobel Prize-winning economist Gary Becker, for example. As a child, my college roommate (later a professor of mathematics) likewise began speaking in complete sentences, as did my computer guru and one of the twin girls in the original group studied in *Late-Talking Children*. The widow of one of the members of Terman's famous high-IQ group wrote to me that he "said nary a word" until he was about three years old and that his first words were a complete sentence: "I think I will do it this way," while assembling something on the floor.[17]

This is only one speech development scenario. Other late-talking children are virtually incomprehensible to most people when they finally begin to speak, though some family members may develop an ability to figure out what they mean. This was the case with famed mathematician Julia Robinson (1919–1985), the first woman to become president of the American Mathematical Society, the first female mathematician elected to the National Academy of Sciences, and winner of a MacArthur Foundation Genius award. When she was a child, Julia Robinson's sister Constance became her interpreter. According to Professor Robinson:

> I was slow to talk and pronounced words so oddly that no one except Constance could understand me. Since people would ask me a question and look at Constance for the answer, she got into the habit of speaking for me, as she is now.[18]

Sometimes a particular event or situation sets the child to talking. One of the mothers in the group I studied was standing at an intersection when one of her silent, four-year-old twin girls suddenly said: "Come on, let's go!" The mother of my computer guru told me that his first words were: "There goes the school bus!" Nationally syndicated talk-show host G. Gordon Liddy was, as a small child, frightened by a huge dirigible that passed low over his house while he was alone in the back yard, eight days before his second birthday. "Screaming in terror," he ran to the door of the house, "pounded hysterically until it opened" and then "I began to speak immediately, to articulate my first memory: absolute, overwhelming fear."[19] Like many other late-talkers, Liddy had a high I.Q., ranging at various times from 137 to 142.[20]

However varied the timing and manner of their speaking, bright children who talk late nevertheless tend to share various personal, as well as intellectual, characteristics. Young Edward Teller was typical of many such children in doing what interested him, when it interested him, but not otherwise. His biographer wrote that "he would play the piano for hours, then he might not go near it for a week." He was also typical of such children in highly uneven development. As an eight-year-old, he worked mathematics problems for fun and played chess with his father, but he still expected his governess to put on his socks for him as she helped him dress.[21]

It is also worth noting young Edward Teller's "refusal" to talk, since this makes a distinction between *inability* and *non-compliance* that many evaluators of late-talking children fail to make, not only as regards talking but also other tasks used to assess children's mental development.

When the child is given some materials and a simple task to perform, but chooses instead to do something more complicated with those materials, some evaluators record this as an inability to perform the simpler task assigned and reach ominous conclusions about the child's mental ability as a result. One little boy who failed to respond to a question as to whether he was a boy or a girl was recorded as not understanding something this basic.

Another late-talking child was pronounced "mentally retarded" after a seven-minute interview in which, among other things, he failed to respond when asked to point to his mother. Many parents of late-talkers report such children's non-compliance when asked to do things that the child has done many times before at home and, more generally, that such children are "strong-willed"—a phrase occurring repeatedly in letters I have received from parents of late-talking children. These children are not "trained seals," as one mother put it. If they are not interested, they don't do it—like Einstein and Teller before them.

Julia Robinson presented a similar picture of herself as a small child:

> My mother, who had taught kindergarten and first grade before her marriage, said that I was the stubbornest child she had ever known. I would say that my stubbornness has been to a great extent responsible for whatever success I have had in mathematics. But then it is a common trait among mathematicians.[22]

A study of geniuses in general characterized creative women as "rebellious and non-conforming,"[23] when compared to women of average ability. Since Professor Robinson found similar characteristics among mathematicians—most of whom are men—this seems to be a tendency among people of high intellectual ability, regardless of sex. However, this trait complicates the evaluation of small children with high intellectual potential, who may not cooperate in the evaluation process.

Separating inability from non-compliance requires judgment, but first the distinction must be recognized as important by the evaluator, who must also be prepared to do more than mechanically go down a checklist. In an age of runaway litigation, blindly following the checklist may be the safest course for the evaluator from a legal standpoint, even if this fails to provide the best evaluation of the child. Personal judgment can be more readily challenged in a court of law than can a widely recognized standard routine in the profession.

When young Edward Teller attended a gymnasium in his native Hungary, he showed disinterest in mathematics at first, not because it was difficult but because what was being taught bored him. This is not an uncommon problem among bright children in general, whether late-talking or not. He also encountered another problem common to bright children, being resented because they are visibly more intelligent than the teacher. After his mathematics teacher, who was also the school principal, demonstrated how to solve an algebraic problem, Teller raised his hand:

> "Is there something wrong, Teller?" he asked, sarcastically. Edward suggested that there was a better way to do it. "Then come up here and do it," said the irritated professor. Edward did, and with more dispatch than his teacher. Oberle's response was to the point: "So you are a genius, Teller? Well, I don't like geniuses."[24]

Nor do mediocre teachers today always like exceptionally bright children—and mediocrities (and worse) abound in our public schools. For bright, late-talking children, such teachers are likely to be a continuing problem, long after these children have mastered speech.

Another public figure who was late in talking was Clara Schumann, a famous concert pianist of the nineteenth century. She was four years old before she began to talk. In later life, she assumed that this was because of a taciturn maid who cared for her and her siblings. However, she had many of the other characteristics found among late-talking children in the groups studied by Professor Camarata and myself, so the maid may not have been responsible, after all.

Clara Schumann characterized herself as "obstinate,"[25] for example, and had a prodigious memory, expressed in the number of musical pieces she could play by heart as a child.[26] Her family was also musical. Her father was a music teacher, her mother was a singer and pianist, her maternal grandfather was a cantor and her maternal great grandfather a distinguished flutist, composer, and manufacturer of musical instruments.[27] By the age of eight, Clara could turn her back to a piano and name which of the keys someone struck.[28]

Talking, however, did not come nearly as easily, and young Clara was also detached from her surroundings, like some other late-talking children.

"I did not begin to pronounce even single words until I was between four and five years old," she said, "and up to that time understood as little as I spoke." She also mentioned "my want of concern in all that was passing around me." This pattern "was not entirely cured" until she was eight years old, "although it improved as I came to speak better and to take more notice of what was going on."[29] This peculiar pattern caused her to be thought to be hard of hearing or "slow" mentally.[30]

At age five, her father began to give Clara piano lessons. By age eight, she participated in a chamber music group at home. As a teenager, she began to give public concerts and, by age eighteen, she was a celebrity in Vienna. As Clara Wieck—before she married composer Robert Schumann—she was enthusiastically received:

> Clara Wieck had arrived in the Austrian capital from her native Leipzig with her father, Friedrich, in December 1837. From her first concert on the fourteenth in the musikvereinsaal to her last appearance in April, when she played for the emperor in the Burg, she was greeted with the kind of adoration the Viennese reserved for artists of the rank of Niccolò Paganini and Sigismund Thalberg. Music lovers fought to buy seats in the over-crowded halls where she played; critics vied with each other in expressions of admiration. At her fourth concert, frenzied applause recalled her to the stage thirteen times. Princes and barons invited her to play at their palaces and showered her with jewels and treasure. The empress herself let her satisfaction be known with a gift of fifty gold ducats. Recalling Clara's reception, Eduard Hanslick, the Viennese critic and music historian, described her as "not a wonderchild—and yet still a child and already a wonder."[31]

One of the internationally renowned pianists of the twentieth century, Arthur Rubinstein, also talked late. Born in Poland in 1877, he began playing the piano at an even younger age than Clara Schumann. The family's piano was bought for his older sisters, but it was little Arthur's to play after his sisters and brothers went off to school:

> The instrument was an upright that his parents had bought when he was about 2 ½ years old, not for him, but for Jadzia and Hela, who were expected to learn to "play a little," like other proper middle-class girls. Instead, the purchase quickly and conclusively decided the fate of the girls' difficult little brother, a late talker who communicated by singing disconnected syllables or wordless tunes.[32]

As Rubinstein himself wrote in his autobiography, as a small child "while nothing would induce me to utter a single word, I was always willing to sing—to imitate with my voice—any sound I heard, thus creating a sensation at home . . . playing the role of a human parrot."[33]

The toddler became fixated on the piano. Whenever he was asked to leave the drawing room where it was kept, he screamed and wept.[34] He began playing the piano at age three.[35] When his father later bought him a violin to play, little Arthur reacted by smashing it, earning himself a spanking. These kinds of strong-willed reactions will be all too familiar to many parents of bright late-talking children.

A month before Arthur Rubinstein's fourth birthday, his uncle wrote to a famous musician of the day, who was also a professor of music, asking him to teach the boy. The professor agreed only to hear him play and evaluate his talent. After hearing the four-year-old play the piano and giving him various tasks to test his abilities, the music professor picked him up, kissed him and gave him a big piece of chocolate. One of these tests was having the boy listen to the professor playing "many tricky chords" and call out the notes involved.

A prodigious memory was another common trait among bright late-talkers shared by Arthur Rubinstein. After hearing a performance of the first suite of Edvard Grieg's *Peer Gynt*, young Rubinstein returned home "to play almost all of it—to the amazement of the family."[36] At this point, Rubinstein was not yet five years old and had not yet begun formal instruction under a professional musician. At age seven, he gave his first public performance.[37] It was the beginning of a career that would last more than eighty years and bring both popular and critical acclaim.

At his death in 1982, the *New York Times* called him "one of the greatest pianists of the century" who was "idolized all over the world."[38] Rubinstein was an extrovert, both in his music and in his social life. Once he and Albert Einstein played a violin and piano duet together, with this result:

> The physicist missed a cue in one passage and came in four beats late. They started again, and once more Einstein missed the cue. Rubinstein turned to his partner in mock exasperation and exclaimed, "For God's sakes, professor, can't you even count up to four?"[39]

PRIVATE INDIVIDUALS

John Sowell

The person whose story is most familiar to me, and who was the reason for my interest in late-talking children in the first place, was my son John. Although he was, in many ways, much like the other late-talking children that I would learn about decades later, at the time I had never seen or heard of anyone like John.

Our first indication that John was very bright came much earlier than any indication that he would be late in talking. He was not yet walking, and was probably not yet a year old, when he first demonstrated an ability to figure out the child locks that we put on folding grates across the doorway to the kitchen and across the open stairwell that led from our upstairs duplex apartment down to the ground floor.

John first figured out the child lock on the grate across the kitchen door and was now able to enter the kitchen at will, whether or not either of his parents was present, exposing himself to all the dangers that a kitchen holds for a small child. I had to replace the child lock on the grate across the kitchen with a more complicated one. After the new lock was installed, John scooted over to it in his little walker and began to study it. Without touching the lock, he stared at it intensely for some time—and then reached out and opened it on the first try!

His skill at figuring out locks caused him to have an accident that could have been serious, but wasn't. He figured out our most complicated lock, the one on the grate across the open stairway. Still in his little walker, John tumbled down the long flight of stairs, crying out in pain and fright, but ending up not seriously hurt.

After he began to walk, John liked to experiment with a door that led out onto a little balcony. When the door was left ajar on warm days, the sunlight reflected off the window panes in the door onto the living room wall, showing the pattern of lattice work in the window. John would examine this pattern on the living room wall closely and then run back to the door to compare it with what he had just seen. Next he would change the angle of the door slightly and run back to the reflection on the wall to see how it had moved also. Then he would change the angle again, and again run back across the room to see how the reflection had moved once more.

After John had done this on a number of occasions, I got my camera and photographed him looking up at the pattern on the wall, smiling in fascination. All this was encouraging, but his first birthday passed without his saying a word. So did his second birthday. When he was about three years old, a few isolated, poorly formed words began to be spoken now and then, but he was clearly not talking—as other children his age and younger were doing in the apartment complex where we lived.

John seemed like a normal child otherwise. He was happy, playful, and got into mischief. Not talking didn't seem to bother him. Whenever he wanted something, he just pointed to it. If he wanted something to eat or drink, he patted the refrigerator. Then, after the door was opened for him, he would point to what he wanted.

Various things happened now and then to indicate that he was not only quite bright, but that he also had a remarkable memory. One day, when John was about three years old, a Presidential speech on television was preceded by the Presidential seal, which filled the screen. Immediately, John ran back into his room and got a Kennedy half-dollar that his grandmother had given him. Then he turned it over to compare the Presidential seal on the back of the coin with what he saw on TV.

Another time, when I was talking on the telephone for a long while, little John seized the opportunity to play with my chess set, which he was forbidden to do. When I came out into the living room and saw the chess pieces scattered all over the floor, I angrily told him to pick them up and put them back where they belonged.

He put all 32 pieces back in their original positions.

Other encouraging things also happened—but at very long intervals, with many discouraging weeks and months of silence in between. It was barely enough to keep hope alive.

Even after John began to say a few isolated words, there were no phrases or sentences. Moreover, it was not clear whether he fully understood the few words he spoke. For example, he said "wah-ee" (water) when he saw a body of water like a pond or a lake, but not when he saw water in a glass or coming out of a faucet.

One night, when I had him with me as I went to the office to get my mail, John pointed to a water fountain in the hall, to indicate that he wanted a drink. This might be a good time to teach him that this was water, I thought.

"Wah-ee," I said to him, pointing to the water coming out of the fountain.

He only became impatient and frustrated that I did not pick him up to get a drink.

"Wah-ee," I repeated, but he only got upset and began to cry.

I picked him up immediately and let him get a drink. He stopped crying—and I began crying.

Although John was taken to medical and other professionals and examined for various possible abnormalities, no one found anything that could explain why he was not talking. Nor did they have any constructive suggestions. Moreover, my trying to teach him to talk got nowhere. He seemed to have no idea what I was trying to do, much less any interest in it. Yet all the things in which he excelled made me unwilling to write him off as mentally retarded, though eventually even his mother told me that I was just being stubborn in not facing reality.

The first helpful suggestions came from a completely unexpected source. At this time, I was an assistant professor of economics, teaching at Cornell University, while continuing to complete the requirements for my Ph.D. from the University of Chicago. Among these requirements was passing language examinations in French and German. Ordinarily, I would have to fly back to Chicago to take these exams. However, at this time a professor of economics from the University of Chicago, the distinguished economic historian Earl Hamilton, happened to be a visiting professor at the State University of New York at Binghamton. I could save the air fare to Chicago by driving down to Binghamton, which was not very far away. Professor Hamilton agreed to give me the tests there.

After I passed my French exam, Professor Hamilton chatted with me and asked how things were going in my life. I told him that things were fine—except that I had a three-year-old son who couldn't talk. A kindly old gentleman, Professor Hamilton asked me many questions about John: Had I taken him to doctors? Did he seem to be bright and alert? After pondering my answers he said to me gently:

"Mr. Sowell, don't try to teach him to talk—not right now. You just give him lots of love and attention. Take him with you wherever you can. Let him know that you think he is the most wonderful little boy in the whole world. And when he feels confident and secure—he'll talk."

Desperate and ready to try anything, I followed Professor Hamilton's advice. Instead of trying to get John to talk, I increased the time I spent with him as much as possible over the next few months. He became visibly happier and more confident.

One day, when he seemed to be in a particularly good mood, I turned on a tape recorder and asked John to say "water."

"Wah-ee!" he cried out. When I played it back for him to hear, he seemed very pleased.

"Rocks," I suggested.

"Rocky!" he cried out. I played that back for him too, and again he looked very pleased at hearing his own voice.

Slowly and bit by bit, I was able to build up his vocabulary. One day, when he was watching the water draining out of the bath tub, I said, "down the drain" and he repeated the phrase—the first time he went beyond speaking a single word at a time. By now, he was just three months away from his fourth birthday.

Nearby Ithaca College had a speech therapy program and John had been on the waiting list for it for some time. Now, after he had begun to speak, our turn finally came. His therapist was a very charming and lovely young lady, which no doubt helped to keep his attention, and she was very good in working with him while his mother and I watched through one-way glass. His speech developed very rapidly.

Like many late-talking children, John was fascinated by music from an early age. One of his favorite Christmas presents was a toy xylophone, on which he learned to play various tunes. While driving across the country, we stayed overnight at a friend's house and I awoke the next morning to the sound of children's tunes being played on a piano. It was John. He had realized that the keys on the piano had the same notes in the same order as those on his xylophone and he began playing his favorite tunes on the piano. Neither his mother nor I played music, so this was his own discovery and his own initiative. Moreover, he had not been taught to read music, so he had to remember the actual sequences of notes for tunes on the xylophone in order to play them on the piano.

My next academic appointment was as an associate professor at Brandeis University. As we prepared to move to Massachusetts, many friends and neighbors came by to say their goodbyes. However, I was surprised to see a lady we barely knew come by as well, bearing a gift. She was the mother of a retarded child and had heard about John from other people in our apartment complex.

"I understand you have a boy like mine," she said, "so I brought this toy that my son likes, and hope that your boy will like it too."

There was nothing to do but thank her for her kindness—and be grateful inside that she was wrong.

As John grew up, he became something of a whiz at math and chess, and later at computers. He never lost his interest in music. As a five-year-old, he began to write down music that he heard in his own improvised system of notes. His toy xylophone had numbers on each panel and John used those numbers to translate music into something that he could put on paper. Often he would fill up an entire page of a notebook with closely packed sequences of numbers, which would enable him to play back these songs and tunes later on.

John also had many of the social characteristics found in the two groups of late-talkers studied by Stephen Camarata and me. He often became absorbed in whatever he was working on or thinking about, becoming oblivious to people and things around him. He also was—and is—stubborn. His family background is also fairly typical of the children in the two groups studied. My brother is an engineer and my father played the piano. John's cousins include two engineers, a high school math teacher, a professor with a Ph.D. in mathematical economics from Princeton, and a girl who was tested for the program for mathematically precocious children at Johns Hopkins. The last two also talked late.

When John was a teenager, his ranking by the U.S. Chess Federation was higher than mine. He took calculus in high school and made an "A." While still in high school, he also worked for two summers as a computer programmer at Stanford University's computer center. Although I was by this time at Stanford's Hoover Institution, he obtained this job independently of me, and in fact I did not even know where the computer center was located, much less know anything about computers.

Like a number of other late-talking children, John was often bored with and alienated from school work, despite doing outstanding work in mathematics and other subjects that caught his interest. He flunked out of the first college he attended, drifted from job to job, and then from college to college. Eventually, John graduated with a degree in statistics and with enough computer courses to begin his career as a programmer. As a hobby, he creates his own computer games.

Richard Rosett

Richard Rosett was born in Baltimore in 1928 and did not speak until he was three years old, when his first spoken word was "melancholy." It was one of a number of words his mother often spoke to him, in hopes of getting him to repeat them. This was simply the one that, for some reason, he finally decided to repeat. Like a number of very bright children, young Dick Rosett disliked school, acted up a lot and got into much mischief. "I was a bad boy," he now says, looking back on that period. However, he liked to read, and in fact often took library books to school and read them when he was supposed to be doing other things. It was not until he reached geometry and trigonometry that he became excited about what he was being taught in school. He was at the top of his class in these subjects. Otherwise, however, high school was a drag for him and he prevailed on his mother to let him drop out and go join the navy.

After returning from the navy, Rosett went back to high school and finished two years' work in one year, doing well in all subjects. Now, with the G. I. Bill to finance a college education, he went off to college—and flunked out of two of them, "highly selective" interests being an academic problem once again. His math professor tried to interest Rosett in becoming an actuary, but others thought he should just leave.

Rosett took a job in New York working on a newspaper. When he met a girl that he immediately fell in love with and wanted to marry, fortunately for him she insisted that he finish college as a precondition. He enrolled in the adult night school division of

Columbia University, where the first course he took was economics—and it ignited his interest in the subject. Now he went on the night shift at his job and enrolled in the regular undergraduate college at Columbia during the day. He majored in economics and never earned less than an A in any subject thereafter.

Richard Rosett was awarded a fellowship to pursue postgraduate study in economics at Yale University, where he earned a Ph.D. in 1957 for an econometric study as his dissertation. He became a professor of economics at the University of Rochester and, later, at the University of Chicago, where he eventually became dean of the graduate school of business. His career also included serving on the faculty of Washington University in St. Louis, where he was also dean of the faulty. In 1990, he became dean of the business school at the Rochester Institute of Technology. His publications, often featuring mathematical economics and econometrics, have appeared in leading scholarly journals.

A Girl Named Leslie

Although *Late-Talking Children* was the first study of a group of bright children with delayed speech development, back in 1974 there was a book about one such child titled *The Slow Speech Development of a Bright Child*. She was a half-white, half-American Indian girl named Leslie, with an IQ of 139, who was "very limited in what she could say" when she was two years old.[40] Leslie exhibited many of the patterns seen in other bright children who talk late.

She had "a remarkable memory" and learned to read almost as soon as she began to talk, at age two. She could count before she was three, as well as being able to draw pictures of people that included eyes, nose, mouth and hair. At age three, Leslie also had an ability to "concentrate on one activity for long periods of time"—for example, sitting at her table for an hour or more, making things with play dough. It was reported that she "works puzzles easily,"[41] like the children in both the Vanderbilt group and in my group. Her language development was not only slow but atypical of normal language development, in that she seldom babbled as an infant. Moreover, when she finally began to vocalize, she experienced "frustration because her family couldn't understand her":

> After a first try, she often took a person by the hand and showed them what she was talking about, if this was feasible. In many instances, there was no way she could make her meaning clear, and she cried or shouted.[42]

Even before she was a year old, and continuing until she was three, Leslie "imitated a number of non-language sounds, such as an airplane overhead, a dog barking, a bird singing, a siren, a fly buzzing, a car starting, or numerous other sounds." She would then look steadily at the person to whom she was addressing these sounds, waiting for a response confirming that they understood what she was conveying—and after receiving that response, she would then resume whatever else she had been doing.[43] Strange as this behavior might have seemed, it was much like that of Arthur Rubinstein as a child, many decades earlier.

Leslie had a musical bent, as with many other bright children who talk late. At age three, she "was able to carry a tune well and enjoyed music." At age four years and eight months, she asked her mother if she could learn to play the piano, after which her mother gave her piano lessons, but only on occasions when Leslie asked for them, rather than on a schedule.[44] It was Leslie's idea, not her mother's. Nor was this musical inclination inherited from her mother, for Leslie was adopted.

The pattern of marching to one's own drummer, found among many bright children who talk late, also applied in Leslie's case, creating problems during her first months in a nursery school class with a teacher with "a highly structured classroom":

> Everyone was required to sit still and do certain things in certain ways at certain times and not speak out of turn. Art projects were pre-drawn and pre-planned for the child to complete. While some children seemed to function well under the stern supervision and constant direction of this teacher, Leslie rebelled, and resorted more and more frequently as time went on to pretending to be a baby or an animal, going around on her hands and knees, making appropriate noises. Her objection was to be some creature who was unable to participate in classroom activities. Her mother took her out of this class and found a more relaxed atmosphere for her where she did very well.[45]

When Leslie first began to talk, it was in whispers, like my son. She continued to speak in low tones when she was unsure of how to say what she was saying[46]—like Einstein before her.

Leslie was also like many other children who talk late but have no trouble understanding what other people are saying:

> There is ample evidence that Leslie was comprehending language. For example, while Leslie repeatedly had difficulty in producing words she needed to express her meanings and relied heavily on multi-purpose words, her passive vocabulary was in the 99th percentile, as evidenced by her score on the Peabody Picture Vocabulary Test.[47]

Yet another way in which Leslie was like other bright children who talk late was that she "did not perform on request." Even after she was talking and was speaking to her puppets, she would not follow suggestions from the investigator as to questions she might ask the puppets:

> With each suggestion from the investigator, Leslie would either look earnestly and silently at the investigator and then go on with her own conversation with the puppets, or she simply ignored the investigator's suggestion entirely.[48]

Leslie's "non-responsiveness to verbal instructions" was a general characteristic of hers. She seldom complied when asked "to do very specific things according to someone else's design."[49] For example, although she had read since age two and was reading to her nursery school class, she balked when asked to read by an investigator.[50]

When this pattern appears in other late-talking children, evaluators going mechanically down a checklist may simply record that the child is unable to perform the task—and from such items dire conclusions may be drawn and labels used that follow the child for years.

Leslie is now grown. She graduated from a prestigious women's college and went on to receive postgraduate degrees at the University of California and the University of Pennsylvania.

A Boy Named Ricky

Ricky was already a teenager and long past the time when he had begun to talk when I first learned about him in September 1993, when our group of late-talking children was being formed.

His mother had contacted me to ask for suggestions of colleges that he might attend. During the course of our telephone conversation, she happened to mention that he was late in beginning to speak and I then urged her to join our group—not for her own sake, but for the sake of other parents of similar children, who take great comfort from being able to have discussions with parents whose children have gone on to do well. On this basis, she agreed to join.

Born in 1979, Ricky was in a number of ways typical of the children in our group. Both his father and an aunt play musical instruments. As a child, he was unusually good at putting puzzles together, his memory was top-rated as "extremely good," and he was late in toilet-training. Unlike most of the other children in our group, however, he was above average in social skills. Since Ricky was one of the older children in our group, his mother did not remember when he spoke his first word or sentence, but she said:

> Ricky was classically slow verbally until about the age of 7 but has obviously no apparent delays now. He is very cerebral and serious. He has a great wit but reserves it for specific moments.

Like many of the other children in the group, Ricky's abilities have been particularly strong in analytical subjects. At age 16, Ricky's PSAT score in math was a hundred points higher than his verbal score—770 and 670, respectively.

As of the time of our 1999 follow-up survey, Ricky was a junior in a leading midwestern university, where he was a varsity athlete and had a 3.9 grade-point average. He has two brothers attending other universities, one of them majoring in music.

Stephen Camarata

As already noted, speech-language pathologist Stephen Camarata of Vanderbilt was himself late in talking. He never received speech therapy, even though he was three and a half years old before he began to speak. People of his generation seldom had "early intervention." Like many other people who talked late, he has no memory of it and learned about it later from his mother:

> I have no memory of learning to talk or comparing my progress to others. I do remember one time in Kindergarten, we were discussing age and I said I was five and another boy said "you are not, you're only four." I wonder if he thought I was four because of my immature language.

Young Stephen Camarata learned more readily from reading than from listening. In the early grades, when so much is taught verbally, he had academic difficulties, but this began to change in junior high school, as more and more teaching and learning was via the printed word. In discussing his younger years in school, Camarata said:

> I remember in the first through third grades thinking that the way to make good grades was to sit quietly in the desk (something I wasn't real good at) and I didn't think it really mattered too much how smart you were. In later grades, the focus is more on reading and math. If a late talker is good in these subjects, they can operate much better because things are much more self explanatory.

Fortunately, things began to change in school:

> I remember in the 8th grade, I made a deal with the history teacher. He gave me the assignments for the whole year. I sat in the back of class (there were probably 45—50 children in a class) and finished that work by thanksgiving (it was workbook stuff and quizzes/tests based on the readings). Then, as long as I kept reasonably quiet, I could do what I wanted. Mostly I read history books and biographies. That was great! In the spring, I had a bad case of mumps and also pneumonia, so I missed about two months of school. I just did

the work at home, so that was great too . . . The work in lower grades is rather narrowly focused and requires the child to closely follow what the teacher is doing (and saying), so it is really about compliance . . . Frankly, I often "tuned out" the instructor's lecture and just completed the assignments on my own (it was easier than listening). In a sense, the more freedom to learn in my own way as school progressed translated to improved performance in school (I was and am a curious person and love to learn new things).

I never had speech or language therapy. Back then (the '60s), speech therapists only focused on articulation problems, stuttering, and voice problems, so no one really paid close attention to language skills as we do today. Therefore, I was never evaluated because my articulation was evidently OK and I didn't stutter. There was a difference in schools too; everyone was simply expected to learn certain basic information. The only special education was for children with pretty severe problems (I remember one neighborhood child we played with who had Downs Syndrome, he went to a different school). So everyone else was put in these large classes . . . 40 or more children . . . and the teachers were expected to teach everyone to read and write and do math. If someone was learning disabled or whatever, they might be held back in a class, but they still had to learn. Now, professionals assign labels to many children and it seems that these labels then allow everyone to have lower expectations for that child. At one school I visited, over 10% of the children came to the office to take medication for hyperactivity. Perhaps it is just easier to deal with children with behavior issues if you medicate them. Anyway, these kinds of labels weren't around when I was growing up, so I never was officially "identified."

As with many other late-talkers, there is both a mathematical and a musical connection. Professor Camarata teaches a graduate course in statistical analysis and, from his grandfather on back for many generations, his forebears earned their livings as musicians.

Other Late Talkers

A letter from a mother in Pennsylvania told the story of her son, who is now in his forties:

> My son at the age of 2¹/₂ years only said my name, Amy. His sister was 14 months younger and began to talk at the age of 15 months. Little by little he began to talk to her and his speech started to develop. My father, who was a physician, insisted that I correct his speech, and I told him that I would be willing to go to a specialist with him, but that I had heard that correcting a child made him nervous. My father arranged for me to take my son to a special clinic where they tested him and then said to leave him alone, that his sounds were coming in slowly. My father more or less wrote this child off as being "slow." In kindergarten he would slide around the table on his belly. For first grade we moved from our rural home to a very good school district and when he came home and told me that he was in the highest reading group, I checked it with the teacher in disbelief. At that time they gave him a group IQ test and said that he was *very, very* average.
>
> At about the age of 12 one of his teachers started to tell me that I should be sending him to college *then*. I then took him to a special guidance clinic and had him tested and found out that he was in the top 1% in intelligence and that only time would tell the limits to his intelligence. Time has proven the guidance clinic correct. I should add that my husband is an engineer with a Ph.D. and now my son is an engineer with a Ph.D. from the University of Pennsylvania who does computer work.

Another late-talker whose intelligence was under-estimated at school is named Jerry Simmons. When he reached high school, Jerry's father suggested that he be put in a program for gifted children, in hopes of resolving his alienation from school. However, Jerry's teachers thought the suggestion absurd in view of his lackluster school work but, after the boy was tested, it was discovered—to his teachers' astonishment—that his IQ qualified him for the gifted program. Once in the program, however, he discovered that it did not offer more challenging work, but just more of the very same work, at the same level, in order to keep the bright students busy. He wrote a letter to the school district superintendent, complaining that it was just more busy work—and he was warned not to do that again.

Frustrated, Jerry turned to his parents and was able to get their permission to drop out of high school after his junior year, by agreeing to take a test for a high school equivalency diploma and go on to college early. Now in a community college, he was able to select challenging courses and did very well in them. He then transferred to a four-year college, where he again did well academically and also became student body president. From there, he went on to law school, where he graduated in 1999 and proceeded on to a postgraduate program in education at Harvard. His plan is to work as an attorney for education reform.

According to Sherman McCall's mother, he did not say more than "Ma" and "Da" until he was four and a half years old. When he was three and a half, his mother wrote in a developmental record she was keeping: "counted cement trucks, still not talking." Like many other late-talking children, he was initially thought to be mentally retarded. When he grew up, however, Sherman McCall scored very high on a variety of tests. He went to Tulane University, where he graduated *magna cum laude* in chemistry, and then went on to get a medical degree. Today, Dr. McCall's record includes various publications, many honors and awards, as well as study, medical and military service, and travel, around the world.

A mother in California wrote to me:

> My second boy uttered no words as his third birthday approached. He hummed and gestured and seemed otherwise normal. The pediatrician was most reassuring; the local speech therapist certainly could offer no help at all. I was desperate but I doggedly continued reading to him and teaching him the alphabets. One heavenly afternoon, waking up from a nap, he started repeating the letters after me and, within the week, he was talking up a storm! He was then three and a half years old.

Today, he is grown and has a doctorate in physics.

The first 30 children in the group I studied were all boys, and girls remained a small minority. As I began collecting examples of adults who had been late-talking children, all of these were men. The first woman I heard of who had talked late was mentioned in a newspaper clipping sent to me from New Hampshire by one of the mothers in our group. The clipping said: "At age 3, she was the little girl who could not talk, not even to form the first, most basic baby sounds, 'mama and dada.'"

"You know how babies coo?" her mother said. "She never cooed."

As of the time I heard about her, this young lady had just graduated from high school—13th in a class of 700. She was going off to college, planning to specialize in engineering. Her father is an engineer.[51]

Eight of the 46 late-talkers in my original study are adults born from 1949 to 1981. For three of them I have Scholastic Aptitude Test scores and for two others I have IQ scores. All three mathematics SAT scores are above the 90th percentile and the two IQ scores are 139 and 180, respectively. (A handful of math SATs that

I have learned about from late-talkers outside our group have also all been above the 90th percentile). Another late-talker in our group, for whom there are neither IQ nor SAT scores available, has a degree in computer science and creates video animations. As children, these particular individuals from my original group began talking as early as age three and as late as age four and a half.

One of these children who began talking at age four and a half is now a middle-aged man. When Kevin turned four, he "made little attempt to talk, only utilizing about seven simple words or tiny phrases when necessary," such as "wah" for a drink, his mother recalled. "Pointing was one method for obtaining what he needed while physical gestures or other variations got him what he wanted."

Like many of the other late-talking children in our group, Kevin was also late to be toilet-trained. He was still wearing diapers at age four—"and never cared whether or not he ever got changed."

Speech therapy rapidly increased his vocabulary in just a few weeks. Still he remained a willful and eccentric child, resisting going to school, not only at first but for years afterward: "School work and grades came real easy for Kevin," his mother said. He didn't have to apply himself and yet "he detested school from that first day until the day he graduated." He "literally counted the days until he would graduate."

At home, Kevin early on demonstrated an ability to take things apart and put them back together again. This also became a way of venting his frustrations. "Any time things didn't go his way," his mother said, he took apart his bed and then re-assembled it, from the frame to the mattress and bedding. Sometimes he took his bed-room door off the hinges and then put it back on again. He was about eight years old when he did these things. As an adult, he became a construction contractor. He became "a finish carpenter," working on homes in the one million dollar and up range.

Kevin's sister had a son who talked late. When Kevin's nephew was 5½ years old, he was still saying "mole ho" for mobile home and "potcays" for pancakes or hot cakes. However, by the time this little boy was in junior high school, he was on the honor roll.

The first of the late-talking children that I heard about from parents who wrote in response to my newspaper column about my son was also named John, but he was born more than a decade earlier. This older John in Missouri had one of the most unpromising beginnings as a young child. He was slow in walking, as well as slow in talking, and he "drooled so that it looked as if I had poured water on the front of his shirt," his mother said.

Although he was "a cheerful child with a bright intelligent look" and could follow instructions, nevertheless friends and relatives suggested that he might someday have to be "put away."

Although John eventually began to say isolated words, he was four and a half years old before he was really talking. Even so, when he went to school, his teachers found his speech hard to understand and questioned his mother as to whether he was normal, especially since he still continued to drool.

When John was eight years old, his mother bought an old piano, so that his older sisters could receive music lessons. Like so many other children in our group, he was fascinated with music. Little John wanted to play the piano himself, but his mother was reluctant to let him, since he was so clumsy. Still, he persisted until he was allowed to try.

His aunt played a tune on the piano and little John then immediately sat down and played it too. By the age of nine, he played the piano in church for a congregation of 2,000 people. He continued to give church recitals until he grew up and went off to join the air force.

After returning home from military service, John was torn between pursuing a musical career and becoming a policeman.

Although he decided to join the police department, he also gave private music lessons on the side, as well as music lessons in local high schools. He has no college degree but does have an IQ high enough to be found in no more than one out of every 10,000 people.[52]

What is both surprising and depressing is discovering how many highly intelligent people have found schools and colleges uninviting, unchallenging and downright irritating and boring. This has not been peculiar to children who talk late. Studies of other very bright children have found similar alienation.[53] Fortunately for those who are now adults, it was not common in their day to call this boredom "attention deficit hyperactivity disorder" and treat it with Ritalin.

Chapter 3

Children Who Talk Late

While adults who once talked late provide some clues to the future development of children with the Einstein syndrome, most late-talkers who have been studied are still children. These include toddlers in Stephen Camarata's group, which began forming in 1997 and is still adding members, while the youngest child in my original group was born in 1992. Although this chapter is anecdotal, the patterns that emerge from these children's stories seem as clear and as striking as the patterns emerging from the statistics in Chapter 1.

The children whose stories follow include children who were not part of either the original group that I studied at the Hoover Institution or the group studied by Professor Camarata at Vanderbilt University. Some of the children whose stories appeared in *Late-Talking Children* have their stories briefly summarized and their subsequent progress updated. Other children from that group have their stories appear here for the first time.

INDIVIDUALS

Braden in Canada

A young Canadian mother wrote of her son, Braden, who was four years old, that he was a "late potty trainer, late talker, early reader, computer literate, his memory is unbelievable"—in short, a classic example of the children in both my original group and in Professor Camarata's Vanderbilt group. His family background also fit the pattern. His grandfather was a chemical engineer, his father received an MBA in finance, and five close family members play musical instruments, including both his parents.

His encounters with professionals and semi-professionals were also classic, though in a negative sense. His mother first became concerned while waiting in a doctor's office for Braden to receive his inoculations at 18 months. She saw a chart showing where a child's progress in speaking should be at that age—and Braden was clearly behind schedule. He was referred to an ear, nose, and throat specialist, who discovered problems in his ears and put tubes in them. "We were told that two weeks after Braden got his tubes he'd be talking," his mother said. "He didn't."

At age two, the little boy was put into speech therapy but "it just upset us and frustrated Braden." He was also put into a day care facility, where one of his teachers "was a huge problem." His mother now says "I should have followed my gut instinct and removed him from there" but instead she followed the advice of his speech pathologist, who said that he needed to be in with his peers. In following this advice, his mother "put my son through eight months of upset." One of the people in the day care center "was convinced that Braden was retarded and couldn't do this and couldn't do that. She was mean, unthoughtful and often reduced me to tears." Like too many people who work with children, this day care worker equated what Braden *wouldn't* do with what he *couldn't* do:

> One day she told me that Braden couldn't climb up the ladder to the change table or step up onto the stool (indicating a physical problem). I told her he *could* do it but *wouldn't* do it for her. She continued on about her concern for Braden's physical development as if I hadn't said anything.

At this point Braden's mother took a toy away from him and put it up on the table in question. Braden then climbed up onto the table and retrieved the toy. Instead of being pleased to discover that the child was all right, the day care worker was irritated that he had proved her wrong. Like my son, Braden was also good at figuring out "child-proof" locks. One day he unlocked a gate at the day care center and the other children began going outside. Although his mother was concerned for the safety of the children, she was also "secretly delighted" that he had both upset the teachers and demonstrated how intelligent he was.

Nevertheless, the people at the day care center continued to doubt his ability—and to express these doubts in his presence. Braden's mother tried to explain to them that her child's understanding of what was said to him was fine, even though he himself did not talk, and that "he did not always do what was asked of him, not because he didn't understand, but because he didn't want to (strong willed doesn't start to describe him)." This too was disregarded and he continued to be regarded as "slow."

Another mother, who happened to be of Chinese descent, stopped Braden's mother outside the classroom and said that in Asian cultures, it was believed that little boys who talk late will be very smart later on. "I remember thinking that whether what she said about Braden was true or false, it was one of the few nice things anyone had said about Braden in a long time, and that little comment was exactly what I needed to hear."

Nevertheless, succumbing to the persistence of the day care people, Braden's mother had him evaluated for possible developmental delay. Although the boy's pediatrician said that he seemed to be fine except for delayed speech development, his mother continued to have misgivings that she had acquired from the day care personnel. She asked for a referral to an audiologist:

> We went to a local audiologist and Braden wouldn't cooperate with what the audiologist wanted him to do. I explained that Braden is an incredibly strong willed child who does not perform tasks simply because they are requested of him, he only does things if and when he wants to. Anyways, the audiologist found his behavior very frustrating and asked me if he was autistic and suggested that maybe I should send Braden to see a behaviouralist. I was furious with the audiologist, but I didn't say anything, it felt like I had just let someone bad mouth my child and did nothing. I drove home crying, wondering if I had been fooling myself, maybe there was something seriously wrong with my son. Now I realize that the audiologist is not qualified to say something like that and should not be listened to. Also, Braden was two years old at the time, how much cooperation did she expect?

The next time he was evaluated, at a local hospital, Braden was just a month away from his third birthday. "The doctor, after seeing Braden for three minutes, said Pervasive Developmental Disorder and that she was going to refer us to the developmental clinic. I felt like someone had punched me in the stomach." The doctor asked if she knew what PDD meant and the mother thought: "OH MY GOD, THEY THINK MY BABY IS AUTISTIC, WHAT AM I

GOING TO DO?" Fortunately, at this point her mother-in-law told her that she had heard of a book called *Late-Talking Children* and told her of a bookstore some distance away where it was available.

> After crying loudly in a public washroom stall (the other women probably though I had lost my job) I took the subway and walked about a mile to the Parents Bookstore. I cried the whole way . . . All the other crises in my life I still had an element of control, I had choices to make. PDD gave me no choice, it's genetic, there's no cure, no vaccination or pills. The most horrible feeling in the world is to think you have a child you will never know. A child who won't share their thoughts and feelings with you. A child you will never talk with. That's what PDD meant to me. I have the burden of caring for and raising this child with none of the emotional benefits of parenting.

Still, she could not reconcile this autistic label with her child's behavior. "Braden was very affectionate, he was always hugging and kissing. One of the few phrases he did say was 'I love you.'" He was so ready to hug that people at the day care center nicknamed him Casanova. Thinking of all this, his mother said, "It just couldn't be PDD. They must be wrong."

After she reached the bookstore and got a copy of *Late-Talking Children*, "I took my new bright yellow book onto the subway for the long ride home, hoping it would somehow erase the PDD mark the doctor had put on my child." She became engrossed in reading about the experiences of other parents with children like her own. She laughed and she cried. Ironically, she had just reached the part where I mentioned how completely absorbed my son or I can become in what we are doing when "I realized that a female voice was repeatedly saying, 'Excuse me.' I looked up and the train was empty. A woman was standing in the doorway, looking exasperated. 'This train is out of service,' she said. 'They announced it on the P.A. system. You have got to get off and wait for the next train.'"

A few days later, when she talked with her pediatrician on the phone, "I asked her how, if she spent only a few minutes with my son, she could have come to the conclusion that he had PDD. She became flustered and said she never said she thought he had PDD. She was just a general paediatrician and was not qualified to make that diagnosis. She said he had some of the symptoms of PDD." Braden's mother became suspicious that doctors were just covering themselves against lawsuits by mentioning worst-case scenarios. "No one is going to be mad that a diagnosis of PDD is retracted, but parents would be very upset if their child had PDD and an overly optimistic doctor missed it, especially with something like PDD where early intervention is key to a child's success." Nevertheless she continued to take Braden around to more medical facilities for more tests. Eventually the little boy became "phobic" about doctors and hospitals. He even grew frightened when taken to a photographer because the photographer had a waiting room, just like the doctors, and had a bright light such as those in examining rooms.

During one medical examination, when a nurse began asking the parents a series of questions, she "asked us if we knew where she was heading with these questions. I told her that it seemed she thought Braden was autistic and she nodded. My husband interjected that Braden is not autistic, he's affectionate and loving, he's sympathetic and his speech is starting to come. He can read, he's amazing on the computer. Then she gave us a sad little smile and asked us, 'Have you ever seen the movie *Rain Man* with Dustin Hoffman?'"

Braden's mother went to another diagnostic center and received an entirely different assessment, including no PDD. "We're still going to continue with the medical testing as I feel it would be irresponsible of me not to, but on the other hand I don't know why I'm putting Braden and us through all this." Like so many parents of bright children who talk late, she is ambivalent. "I still have my days where I'm worried about what could possibly be wrong with Braden and I have days when I'm not worried about him at all."

Jonathan in New York

Jonathan was five years old when his mother first wrote to our group in December 1994. She said: "I tried my best at 2 ½ to get him to speak, but failed." Even now, at age five, he was having "great difficulty putting more than three words together." His general level of speech was estimated as being that of a child two-and-a-half to three years old. Preschool personnel labeled him a high-functioning autistic child with "pervasive developmental disorder" (PDD). A Yale psychiatrist and a neurologist disagreed with this diagnosis. Still, his mother said: "So here I am, afraid he'll never be 'normal' or be able to get on in the world."

Nearly two years passed before she wrote again. This time she reported "incredible progress." Nevertheless, the local authorities in the school system remained fixated on the PDD label. Another two years later—now December 1998—she wrote:

> I can't believe how far he has come . . . He is now in the third grade and I can't believe he couldn't talk or understand us at four. . . . He now plays chess, is a math whiz and has a nice group of friends he hangs out with. . . . I threw out any information I had on autism or PDD.

At the time of the follow-up study in July 1999, Jonathan's mother reported "an enormous leap in understanding language" during the school year just ended. He was now "super social" as well as "a super smart student." His speech still "sounds odd" and he was found to have some hearing problems, but he "talks about very complex things and also social things."

Like so many of the children in both groups studied, Jonathan was musically inclined. He plays cello in the school orchestra. His siblings likewise fit the family profiles seen among the relatives of bright children who talk late. His older half-brother holds a master's degree in fine arts and supports himself by working part-time in the computer field. His sister won a New York state award in the seventh grade for a Scholastic Aptitude Test score above 1100— higher than that of the average college student. She took the test as part of the Johns Hopkins University program for intellectually precocious children. She also won an award for playing the violin.

In retrospect, Jonathan's mother says that she "worried too much" about his late talking, "suffered emotionally when I was told he had PDD," and "feared he'd never lead a normal life." Her views, however, were "very different" from those of his father, who was "optimistic" even during those difficult early years.

Billy in California

When Billy was two and a half years old and still not talking, his parents had him evaluated by a series of professionals—a pediatrician, an audiologist, a speech pathologist, and a developmental psychologist. These professionals' conclusions were as different from one another as those of various relatives who had seen Billy. The diagnosis that jolted the parents was the psychologist's "pervasive developmental disorder"— part of the autism spectrum. But the speech pathologist thought otherwise. A questionnaire that the parents obtained from the Autism Research Institute likewise did not indicate autism.

As with so many children on whom the "pervasive developmental disorder" label was put, Billy's development was at least normal—and in some ways more advanced than normal—in a number of areas, so there were no "pervasive" problems. He had crawled when he was 6 months old, was standing a week later and walked before he was 11 months old. He could ride a tricycle at 18 months and could use a videocassette recorder and a computer when he was two and a half years old, as well as do puzzles designed for four-year-olds. He just did not talk.

Like so many other bright children who talk late, Billy would not perform on cue, which made it difficult for others to evaluate him or to teach him. His parents were of course very worried, as well as confused by the conflicting opinions they encountered. Billy's pre-school teacher was likewise concerned because he did not speak and because he seemed not to understand what she was saying to him. Moreover, Billy's own frustrations in being unable to make himself understood led to long tantrums. However, he could also be very affectionate and loved to be held and cuddled, which was very different from the behavior of autistic children.

Billy's speech emerged in a very sporadic fashion. Even before he was a year old, he would imitate some sounds, such as "mama" and "dada." But these were just sounds, rather than real words that he used to convey meanings. His first meaningful words were "No, mama"—used just one time, when he was 15 months old, when his mother was taking away a vacuum cleaner that he was interested in. It was about a year and a half later before he made another two-word statement. He was three years old before he would say short sentences, such as "I want —" Back and forth conversation did not begin until his fourth year, and then only with great efforts on his parents' part to draw him out.

Even before he was four years old, Billy knew which of his computer games were in Windows and which were in DOS, and he could access both without any help. Like other children in our group, his memory was found to be "astounding" in his mother's words. Still, his parents were haunted by the differing assessments of him that they had received.

"Due to the conflicting messages we have been receiving," his mother wrote, "we are left to trust to our own instincts. It is hard to do that, when you are not a trained professional and the professionals tell you that you are in denial!" When Billy's parents sought a second opinion, no one would give them one "without a referral from our pediatrician or reading the report from the psychologist." Realizing how this would defeat the whole purpose of getting an independent evaluation, his parents wanted no part of this. Eventually, however, they did find another speech therapist who concluded that Billy did *not* need the sort of therapy recommended by others. Moreover, this therapist said that the clinic that Billy had been to was notorious for "over-diagnosing" children.

Nevertheless, Billy's parents were not yet prepared to reject the psychologist's diagnosis of "autism" and followed her advice to enrol their son in a program for autistic children and to themselves become part of a support group of parents with autistic children. Eventually, one of the other parents in the support group took them aside and said that she had been watching Billy—and that he didn't seem at all like the autistic children he was with. A preschool teacher who was allowed to come observe Billy in this group of autistic children was even more emphatic. In fact, she went ballistic and exclaimed: "TAKE HIM OUT OF HERE! THEY ARE GOING TO UNDO ALL OF THE PROGRESS WE HAVE MADE WITH HIM!"

Now Billy's mother turned against the "experts" who had misdiagnosed him. Moreover, Billy himself was growing more hostile to the therapy and testing sessions. In addition, his teachers pointed out that Billy did better at school on days when he did *not* have speech therapy.

In preschool, Billy was very attached to a little girl named Heidi. They became inseparable at school and he talked about her incessantly at home. Unfortunately, Heidi's parents divorced and she went back and forth between her father and mother every two months. When she was gone, Billy played by himself or briefly with other children. When she came back, she was put in a different class. But when Billy saw her on the playground, he ran over to her and said to the other children: "*My* Heidi." Despite all this happening before their eyes, those who considered him autistic did not change their minds, and one teacher used strained interpretations of words to say that he and Heidi were not really "interacting."

Such dogmatism took a dangerous turn when a pediatrician was told about some strange behavior that Billy was developing. Billy began to keep one eye closed—sometimes the left, sometimes the right—and eventually reached the point where he would never have both eyes open at the same time. When his mother phoned his pediatrician to ask for a referral to an ophthalmologist, the pediatrician seemed confident that this odd behavior was not an eyesight problem—and Billy's mother exploded in anger. She told him that, if Billy had not been given a label, he would be recommending an eye exam.

The pediatrician finally agreed to give a referral to a pediatric ophthalmologist who has "worked with kids like Billy." This ophthalmologist had in fact worked with autistic children—and he said that Billy did not act like one of them. The problem was that Billy had double vision, easily corrected with glasses if caught in time, but a danger to lead to blindness in one eye if not corrected.

After his eye problems were corrected, Billy's behavior improved in many ways, as his ophthalmologist had predicted. His parents saw it at home and his teachers reported similar improvements at school, where his idiosyncracies had been a continuing problem before. Billy was so advanced on the computer that he could help his mother or his preschool teacher when either of them had problems with Windows 95. Family and friends were now also commenting on his progress in social development.

In addition to what his parents and teachers have taught him, Billy has figured out other things on his own. His mother was amazed to have him explain Roman numerals to her when he was seven years old. Although he had never been taught Roman numerals at home or at school, and did not even know that this was what they were called, he had seen them on a clock and figured out how the position of the individual characters determined whether the numbers they represented were added or subtracted. His mother was astonished.

In early 1996, when I was taking a survey of the group while writing *Late-Talking Children*, Billy's mother reported his continuing progress and the fact that he was now playing the piano. Like other children in our group, he has taken to music very readily. He liked to show off by playing the piano with his eyes closed. Eventually, he began to give local recitals at age seven. For one of his recitals at age eight, he learned a new song that he liked and wanted to substitute for the program that was planned. His piano teacher told him that he could, but only if he learned it in time. He came home that night and "and was obsessed with playing it over and over"—until midnight, when his parents made him go to bed. Here again, we see the pattern of self-driven concentration found in other very bright children who talk late.

Billy's academic progress remained highly varied—way ahead in some things and way behind in others. The same was true in athletics, where he was completely "clueless" in basketball for a very long time, standing out on the court like a sore thumb for his ineptness—and then, after finally getting the hang of it, becoming a star player on his team.

Billy's parents re-arranged their lives to give him the best chance of developing. His mother quit working and his father found a job in another community where they could live on one salary. In addition, they spent time and money on various programs designed to improve his verbal skills and general development. Whether because of all these things or otherwise, Billy's improvement was at a very gratifying pace. His teachers, as well as his parents, have seen it.

Billy was told that he was going to have a baby sister and was very excited at the prospect. No doubt it would no longer be possible for his parents to continue to lavish as much time and attention on him as they had, but perhaps he had reached the point where that would no longer be necessary.

Billy's social development, which had been rated below average for 1996, was by 1999 rated as borderline average. "He seems to get along much better with much older kids," his mother says. Other studies show that this is common with very bright children in general.

At school, Billy "excelled in math in particular," his mother wrote. The teacher in his second grade class liked to give the children third-grade math problems, which he did not expect them to solve, but which he could use to show them how to go about figuring them out. Billy seldom seemed to be paying attention to the teacher's solutions, but was able to solve the problems anyway. According to his mother:

> In one case, the teacher got an answer wrong and after Billy corrected him and the teacher discovered Billy's answer was right, he had Billy show the class how he had solved the problem. Billy loved these problems and in his progress report the teacher claimed that Billy often asked for more problems to solve.

One of the continuing areas of difficulty for Billy has been writing. However, in March 1999, "Billy's writing started to improve by leaps and bounds." Moreover, this happened "at a time when no one was paying much attention. His teacher believed that he was just "ready." When Billy reached the third grade and was given standardized tests, he ranked in the 99th percentile in mathematics.

Like many other children in our group, Billy likes to construct things and is very good at it. At age seven, for example, he put together by himself a model roller coaster set designed for teenagers. In the summer of the year 2000, his mother wrote: "Since Emily was born, there have been things that we bought to use for her, and when we'd open the box, Billy would exclaim 'Yes!!! Assembly required!!!!!' He gets very excited to see those words and can usually put together whatever it is for me, without any problem."

"He's made a lot of growth these past few years," his mother said. "Sometimes it is hard to believe we ever worried about his development."

Twins in Alabama

Amy and Laura are identical twins who were born in 1986 and live in a small town in Alabama. Delayed speech development was just one of their problems. They did not interact socially with other children in kindergarten or with their teacher, and were unruly and aggressive. Like other children in our group, they were late in toilet training and stubborn. Some of their behavior— walking on their toes, gazing at their hands, and beating their backs against walls—are recognized characteristics of autistic children, but their pediatric neurologist declared that they were not autistic. Others, including teachers and some family members, thought they were.

The girls also had strengths, however—and these were much like the strengths of the boys in our group. By the time they were two and a half years old, the twins could identify numbers up to 20 and recite the alphabet, as well as identify letters in random order. They readily mastered such electronic equipment as computers and videocassette recorders. Although the youngest children in their kindergarten, they were also characterized by their teacher as "the smartest in the class." However, their misbehavior caused their parents to be asked to take them out of kindergarten.

Two of the things that caused the most concern early on—delayed speech development and autistic kinds of behaviors—tended to improve over the years, but their misbehavior continued to make normal placement in a regular classroom an elusive goal.

A breakthrough in speech came unexpectedly when the four-year-old twins were out strolling with their mother one day and paused at a street corner.

"Come on, let's go," Amy said. A couple of months later, Laura also began to talk. The girls spoke in short phrases. As time went on, these lengthened into six to eight-word sentences. Toilet-training likewise developed unexpectedly after years of futile efforts by the parents. Autistic behaviors had declined considerably, especially for Amy, though Laura continued to have disproportionately strong emotional responses to daily problems.

After the twins entered regular school, their parents were forced to fight a series of battles with various officials over the proper placement of the girls, who required special classes. While the schools have tended toward day care kinds of classes, the parents have pushed—usually unsuccessfully—to get more academic material into their curriculum.

Amy and Laura received a certain amount of home-schooling by their parents to supplement their meager academic work in their special education classes. They have mastered more challenging work at home than they were being given at school. However, telling the school officials this or showing them the work done by the girls at home made no impression.

Over the years, both parents have made extraordinary efforts for their children— not only going to battle with school evaluators and risking legal trouble by keeping them home when the class the girls were placed in was intolerable. At one point, when the girls found a good school environment, they had to spend 3 hours a day on busses to and from the school, until their father decided to drive them one way, though this meant a three-hour round-trip for him every day.

As of the time of the follow-up survey in 1999, the twins were entering their teens still in "special education" classes and were now on medication to control their misbehavior. They were separated into different classes and the class for Laura was described by their mother as one where the primary objective was "just making it through the day." By this time their father had died of a heart attack.

The girls' use of language was now "greatly improved," their mother said:

> They both communicate regularly in a back and forth manner, in complete sentences. Only occasionally will they use a wrong pronoun or verb tense. I usually just point it out briefly and ask them what the correct way would be, and they correct it themselves.

On mental tests, the girls scored within the normal range as of the time of the 1996 survey, but had dropped below it by the time of the 1999 follow-up study. How much of this represented a real measure of their mental development and how much it reflected other factors, including perhaps the death of their father, cannot be known at this point.

The twins' social skills are now rated "below average" but that is still a step up from the "far below average" that their mother gave them in 1996. How things will turn out in the future is far less certain than the extraordinary dedication and fortitude their parents have shown on their behalf thus far. There is also another child in the family, a year older than the twins. His best subject is math.

Andy in New York

Andy was not quite four years old when his mother joined our group in 1996. She had learned about the group from the Internet, where she encountered another mother of a late-talking child who was already a member.

Despite half-hour speech therapy sessions, four times a week, Andy was still not talking and his mother was very worried. She flew out to Texas to talk with the other mother she had met on the Internet. "We spent the weekend talking and crying about our children's future," she said. Afterwards, the mothers e-mailed each other regularly and sometimes phoned as well. Later the mother in Texas flew to New York for a visit.

As of the time of the spring 1996 survey of the group, Andy had still not spoken a complete sentence or engaged in back-and-forth conversation, though he was now four years old. Just hearing him say isolated words was "music to my ears," his mother said. However, she added: "I still worry when and if the ability to have a conversation will occur." This was written on August 12, 1996. Just two weeks after these melancholy thoughts, she wrote again: Andy was starting to speak! She greeted each step toward fluent speech "with a sigh of relief."

Ironically, it was only after the speech therapy sessions stopped that Andy began saying more than isolated words. Andy's mother was thoroughly disgusted by the particular therapists he had had, whom she characterized as insensitive, rude and nasty. After the therapy ended, his mother said that there was "more progress in the last four months than at any other time." She said: "I feel that between the age of 3 and 4 we lost an entire year of potential speech" because the particular speech therapists who worked with him "held him back."

Delayed speech was not Andy's only problem. Misbehavior at home, and especially at school, was marked also by sly manipulativeness and testing the limits of what he could get away with.

A year later, in the summer of 1997, publication of *Late-Talking Children* was followed by media interest. "Dateline.NBC" interviewed some members of our group, including both Andy's mother and her friend in Texas. When the program was finally broadcast in March 1999, it featured the boy in Texas, who was now also making great progress.

When Andy's mother responded to the 1999 follow-up survey of our group, she wrote:

> I am so happy and proud to finally be able to say Andy has really progressed in the last 3 years. His speech, although not on an average 7-year-old level, has improved greatly. He is speaking in full sentences which can be anywhere from 7 to 12 words in length. He is asking appropriate questions and can answer mine.

Now Andy's mother became aware of his remarkable memory, which "constantly amazed" her. There was also a musical connection of sorts: When Andy's older brother played a trumpet for a year, Andy "loved hearing Steven practice and would hum along in the right keys."

One problem remaining was Andy's misbehavior, especially at school. But this is a problem with all too many other children, regardless of when they begin to speak.

Hayley in Arkansas

Hayley was born in 1990 and her mother first wrote to our group shortly before her fifth birthday in 1995. Like a number of the children in our group, she is good-looking enough to be a model.

Hayley said nothing—not even "mama"—before she was three years old and then began saying only a few single words. She was in speech therapy even before she turned three. She barked like a dog. She would also "throw horrible temper tantrums when she did not get her way."

By the time her mother contacted us, Hayley was able not only to say words but to communicate what she wanted. Like many of the boys in our group, she was very good at putting puzzles together and had a memory described as "exceptionable" and "photographic." Her teacher "has commented several times that she has never seen a child with that kind of memory." Her mother also called her (in all capital letters) STRONG WILLED.

Hayley's family also fits the profile of the children in the group. Five close family members, including her mother, play musical instruments and her older sister is described as "very good in math and science." Her mother is a science teacher.

Some people thought that Hayley was autistic—and these included her mother. However, when she was evaluated at a children's hospital, the conclusion was that she was definitely *not* autistic. However, it was thought that she might have a mild case of pervasive developmental disorder, as well as attention deficit hyperactivity disorder and, of course, speech disorder. They put her on some medication. Her mental age was judged to be below her chronological age. But, when she was re-evaluated three months later, her IQ had risen 44 points. This may say more about the variability of the child's responses at different times than about actual changes in mental ability over such a short span.

As of 1999, Hayley's mother reported that she "has progressed tremendously." Now nine years old, she was described as "an avid reader" with a remarkable vocabulary and someone who watches the nightly news, as well as becoming a *Titanic* buff and memorizing most of the bones in the human body. "She is just not interested in the normal 9 year old stuff," her mother says. In school, her test scores put her at or above grade level in mathematics, spelling and reading. Nevertheless, she does not make as high grades as her mother considers her capable of making. She could be a straight-A student, her mother believes, but very bright youngsters are often not conventional enough to get straight A's.

Hayley's social skills have been described as "not quite where they should be" and she as "a loner." Her mother arranges various social activities for her—softball, Girl Scouts, gymnastics—not for their own sake but to get her interacting with other people. "If I did not take her to these things," her mother says, "she would stay in her room all the time." However, her social skills, which were rated "far below average" in 1996, are now rated "average" —a big step up, like her other advances.

Lee in Texas

Lee is a girl who was born in 1991. Her mother first contacted our group in February 1995, as a result of someone's having sent her a copy of a newspaper column of mine about late-talking children. Both she and her family fit the profile. Her father is a computer programmer, her grandfather is an engineer, and an uncle is an accountant. She was not only late in talking but also late in potty training and her memory was described as "unbelievable." She was also musically inclined, being able to "baby talk many, many songs long before she could actually talk." When asked about Lee's fascinations, her mother wrote: "Music—loved it from an early age." Lee is an only child and "the light of my life," her mother said.

Lee said her first word—"mama"—before she was a year old, but she was three and a half before she made her first statement using more than one word and was four and a half before she began to speak in complete sentences or engage in back and forth conversation. As with many of the other children studied, Lee could not be successfully examined when she was first evaluated at age two. The whole thing was described as "extremely" stressful and she was crying. As of age five she showed progress but her parents were told that she would never catch up to her age level.

Like one of the other children in our group—now a middle-aged man—she drooled "constantly" and, like Billy in California, she had eye problems that led an ophthalmologist to suspect that she "uses only one eye at a time, and consequently probably has very poor depth perception." She began to wear glasses at age five and her eyes were operated on when she was between seven and eight. She was also operated on for a cleft palate. In the months following the palate surgery, her speech "improved greatly." Her mother added:

> . . . her vocabulary is out of this world. The words are coming out
> faster than I can keep up with. It's wonderful!

Lee's mother rated her daughter's social development as below average as of 1996 and above average as of 1999. She has "come a long way—much calmer, has a *very* outgoing personality." She still tests below grade level in school "but had the biggest leap in progressing ever" in the year before the 1999 follow-up study.

This was one of those situations where the two parents viewed the child's development very differently—so differently that the mother left with her child when Lee was six and a half years old. "It was truly the best things I could have done for both of us—she has really blossomed."

Luke in Arkansas

Luke's mother was among the first parents to write to me after my newspaper column about my son appeared in May 1993, shortly after her son turned three. At that point, Luke spoke mainly in single syllables, though occasionally he spoke two words together. He understood what was said to him but said little in return.

Although it is usually the mothers who write about the children in our group, both parents wrote about Luke. They were very apprehensive and confessed, "our hearts are heavy," though Luke himself was "a very happy child." He communicated his wants in imaginative, non-verbal ways. According to his mother, "Luke has an excellent memory and does great with puzzles and objects that fit or stack together." He was also late in toilet training and threw tantrums, "without a word, except for crying and an occasional 'no.'" "Like so many bright children who talk late, Luke would often concentrate intently on whatever happened to interest him—whether a toy, a video or whatever—and ignore whatever other activity or people might be around.

Luke's family was also very much like the families of other children in the groups studied. His father and an uncle are Certified Public Accountants, his grandfather is an engineer, and another uncle is a physician. His mother, grandmother, grandfather, and an aunt all played musical instruments, and his little sister has learned to play both the violin and the piano.

Luke was put into speech therapy, which helped some, but it also brought a devastating message to his parents from the therapist: She thought he was autistic. It was "a bombshell" to them. Fortunately, when they took their son to other professionals, these others all agreed that he showed no signs of autism. Indeed, the boy's physician was indignant that someone with no medical qualifications would dare to make such a diagnosis.

Shortly after Luke's fourth birthday in April 1994, his father wrote to the group, reporting on his progress. In six months, Luke's vocabulary had more than doubled, his pronunciation was improved, and now he spoke in two to three-word sentences, though he still had pronunciation problems. However, he was not yet conversing back and forth, as his younger sister (2½ years old) did.

By the time of our 1999 follow-up survey, Luke's father wrote:

> We have wonderful news! Luke is progressing very well in school, without any in-class assistance, and his social skills are steadily improving. Luke excels in math and his reading is average but getting better every day.

While Luke's report card for the academic year just ended then (1998–99) showed varied results in different subjects, he was straight A in math.

Other Children

One mother wrote to me about her little girl who would say absolutely nothing in school, not even to children she knew in the neighborhood, but she started to talk to them after she was on the bus returning home and she talked readily once she was home. Although this is a rare situation, it occurs often enough to have a name—"selective mutism." A grandfather whose grandson was not speaking at all overheard the little boy saying words to himself in the back yard when he thought that he was alone. Leslie, the little girl mentioned in Chapter 2, also did this, practicing the word "vanilla" until she felt confident enough to say: "Mom, listen to me. I got a vanilla bar."[1]

Another mother of a child who refused to talk wrote to me:

When my son began kindergarten his teacher was very, very worried. After his being in school for a couple of weeks she approached me.

"Angela", she said, "I think we need to test Cary." You see, he had not spoken not even one word to her, the aide, or any other student. Even when asked a direct question, he refused to speak. He would point.

"What is your name?" He would walk to his desk and point to his name tag taped on top.

"What color crayon do you want?" He would point. They had tried to tell him that, if he didn't speak it out loud, then he would not get the crayon. He would shrug and walk back to his desk and just watch the other kids.

The teachers were beside themselves with worry. Never in their whole teaching careers had they had a child that wouldn't talk even one word. "Must test!" were the words I heard for months. I kept telling them there was nothing wrong with my son; he spoke at home, therefore I knew he could speak.

"Leave him be," I said. "He will speak when he is good and ready." However, the teachers insisted I was delaying his development by not getting him TESTED!

The Christmas break came and the school began again in January. After two weeks the teacher said, "Angela, what happened to Cary?" Now she was worried because he wouldn't shut up!

Another mother was much more worried. However, she discovered that her little boy began to talk more readily after she stopped trying to teach him to talk or to evaluate his speech. "I see now that my anxiety played a part in hindering his development," she said.

Yet another mother of a late-talking child wrote to me of his strong attraction to music. As a toddler, he became deeply absorbed in listening to Bach, to the point of being moved to tears. A study of gifted children likewise reported: "One three-year-old sat raptly through a three-hour opera on TV, yet was unable to sit through one program of *Sesame Street*."[2] This also has implications for the restlessness of many high-IQ children in school. Such children may get labelled "hyperactive" or as having an "attention deficit disorder," when in fact they are simply bored by the low level of school work—and might be fascinated by something more in tune with their interests and abilities. Unfortunately, there is much more readiness to medicate such children than to give them more challenging work that would engage their abilities.

Far from being inclined to adjust to outstanding intellectual abilities that some children have, educators with a lockstep view of how every child should develop have expressed alarm at some late-talking children who read much earlier than other children. There is even a term for it, as if it were a disease—"hyperlexia." Genuine hyperlexia involves precocious reading *without comprehension*, but that proviso can get lost in the shuffle when low-level semi-professionals make these assessments. It is not uncommon for bright children who talk late to read early. As already noted in Chapter 2, Leslie learned to read "almost as early as she learned to talk," which was around age two.[3] Professor Winner's study of high-IQ children in general likewise found early reading to be common among them:

> Early reading is a reliable sign of high IQ; not only did the group as a whole read far earlier than average, but IQ differences within the group also predicted age of reading. Those with IQs above 170 were over twice as likely to have read before four than were those with IQs below 170.[4]

Nevertheless, some educators and evaluators are quick to label a child "hyperlexic," especially if that child is also late in talking. But being inarticulate does not mean that the child does not understand what he reads, merely because he cannot yet express that understanding in words.

One mother accidentally discovered that her son could read when he automatically turned right at a sign in a hospital that said for children to go to the right and adults to the left. When she asked how he knew which way to turn, he simply pointed to the sign. Other practical written instructions could be devised to test whether an inarticulate child understands what he reads—but only if there is serious consideration being given to going beyond a mechanical checklist when evaluating children.

SOME GENERAL THOUGHTS

The themes of music, math, and memory recur with the children in this chapter, as with the adults in Chapter 2. Where the child is too young for math, such things as precocious skill in putting puzzles together suggests a similar analytical bent. Another and more negative theme is the tendency of some "experts" to jump to conclusions and then to dismiss any information from the parents or evidence from the child's own behavior that goes against their pat conclusions.

"Pervasive developmental disorder" seems to be especially fashionable as a diagnosis, even when the child's problem is limited to delayed speech development and he or she is at least average, or even above average, in other development. Nor do the educational or medical systems seem to have any procedures in place to monitor how often their diagnoses have turned out to be wrong, so that they might at least become less dogmatic in the future. There is another term—"specific language impairment"—which applies to children whose sole problem is that their speech development is delayed, but with "no obvious accompanying conditions such as mental retardation, neurological damage or hearing impairment."[5] How often this label would apply more aptly than PDD is a question that can hardly be asked, much less answered, so long as diagnoses are not systematically checked against the future course of a child's development. Professor Camarata's research project at Vanderbilt University, which will follow the same late-talking children for years, may provide a rare opportunity to put many PDD diagnoses to the test.

When a child's speech becomes normal and his or her other development belies the original diagnosis, the parent may simply stop consulting the "experts." How much good it would do to let the professionals know that their diagnosis turned out to be mistaken seems problematical, given some professionals' tendency to dismiss whatever parents say and to label parents as being "in denial" whenever the diagnoses are questioned. It might in some cases be more fitting to say that it is the professionals, and especially the semi-professionals in the schools and elsewhere, who are in denial as to the many uncertainties remaining at the current state of knowledge in this complex area.

Not all the stories in our group have had happy endings. At least one of the children's diagnosis of autism has stuck and a few others still have serious problems, not to mention a couple of families from whom nothing is heard anymore and whose children's outcomes can only be surmised. On the whole, however, most of the children in my group have emerged not only more verbal than their parents would have expected, but also showing remarkable abilities for their age and even significant improvement in social relations over the years. There is no reason to assume that every single child in my group—or in Professor Camarata's group—represents the pattern of the Einstein syndrome. What is remarkable is how many do.

While it is good to know what has happened in the lives of many bright children with delayed speech development, what we would really like to know is why this unusual condition exists in the first place and what parents can do about it. Preliminary attempts to deal with these questions will be made in the next three chapters.

Chapter 4

Groping for Answers

No one really knows the answer to the baffling question that so many parents, as well as medical and other professionals, ask themselves: Why is a child who is so obviously bright, in so many ways, unable to talk when other children begin talking?

What is known, however, is that there are a number of other anomalies that are far more common among children with high IQs, or children who are musically gifted, than in the general population. Left-handedness and childhood myopia, as well as allergies and other immune system disorders, are all more common among high-ability people than among people of average ability. There is even a name for such phenomena: "The pathology of superiority."[1]

By and large, people with high IQs are healthier than the general population, even though they are more prone to particular abnormalities. That makes these abnormalities all the more puzzling.

Members of the high-IQ Mensa society, for example, show much higher incidences of allergies than in the general population.[2] More than half of a group of very intellectually precocious children studied at Johns Hopkins University also had allergies, this incidence being more than twice the frequency found in the general population.[3] Childhood myopia is also much more common among very bright children—about four times the normal rate in one study.[4] A study of musically gifted individuals found them to have twice the rate of certain learning disabilities found among other people in the same study.[5] Mathematicians and top-rated chess players have a higher than average incidence of left-handedness and/or ambiguous handedness.[6]

Johns Hopkins University has long had a program for very intellectually precocious children—for example, 12-year-olds who can score 700 or better on the mathematics SAT. A sample of such children showed that more than four-fifths of them were myopic and/or allergic and/or left-handed.[7]

Against this background, it may not be quite so surprising that there are also some very bright children who are late in beginning to speak. None of this, however, tells us why these things are correlated. Nor is anyone certain. But researchers who have studied the brain have suggested reasons why certain anomalies are more common among highly intelligent people.

THE BRAIN

The brain controls many things besides the intellect and the emotions. Among these things are the immune system and the optical system, as well as both the voluntary and involuntary use of various other parts of the body. Moreover, different parts of the brain control different things—the right hand, for example, being controlled from the left hemisphere of the brain. While all brains are not organized in exactly the same way, there are certain general patterns as to locations from which particular functions are usually controlled. For example, in about 95 percent of right-handed people, speech is controlled from the left hemisphere, as is also true for about 60 percent of left-handed people.[8]

The size of brain areas controlling different functions can also vary with the degree of proficiency in that function or with the frequency with which that function is performed. People with perfect pitch, for example, have been found to have a specific region of the brain physically larger than that in most other people.[9] Musicians who play string instruments likewise have a region of the brain that is physically larger than normal.[10] So do people who read braille.[11] When Einstein's brain was autopsied, it was found to be no heavier than a normal brain, but one region of his left hemisphere was twice the normal size.[12]

The direction of causation is not always clear—whether the greater use of particular skills causes the corresponding area of the brain to develop more than usual or whether it was first the unusual development of a particular region of the brain that caused the individual to have a higher level of particular skills. Nevertheless, research has shown such correlations.

Modern, high-tech methods of tracking brain activity show that there are also differences between the sexes in the way brains are organized and function, with men's brains generally having more localized and specialized regions for doing particular kinds of thinking, while women are capable of using more parts of the brain simultaneously for a given kind of thinking. Females are thus better able to recover from localized brain damage, because undamaged regions may take over the functions formerly performed in the injured area. More specifically, research has shown that women recover the use of language after strokes and brain surgery more readily than men do.[13] Even under normal conditions, the brains of women and men function somewhat differently when talking.[14]

For both sexes, regional specialization within the brain is less pronounced in early childhood. At that time, there are cells or networks in the brain that can be organized to be used either for one particular function or for some other function. Put differently, as the various functions of the brain develop in infants and toddlers, the corresponding regions compete for resources that have not yet become as specialized as they will be later on.

In some people, that early competition can result in the intellectual functions of the brain getting a disproportionately large share of the resources and some other function or functions ending up with skimpy resources. The net result, according to neuroscientists who support this hypothesis, can be very smart people who are very susceptible to allergies, for example, because that part of the brain which controls their immune system does not get enough resources to cope with all the irritating things in the environment.[15]

Childhood myopia, which once was thought to be due to brainy children doing a lot of reading, has now been determined to be predominantly, if not totally, hereditary.[16] The optical system, like the immune system, requires considerable resources that it simply may not get when intellectual regions of the brain take more than their usual share. That may be why childhood myopia is much more common among precociously intelligent children.

Because of the proximity of the region of the human brain controlling the operation of the right hand and the region used in the kind of thinking required for mathematics, chess, and other highly analytical activities, some people with unusual analytical abilities may have gotten this level of ability by a disproportionate development of a region of the brain that takes resources normally used in making the right hand more skilled than the left. Like most things human, this need not apply in every case. Most mathematicians and top chess players are right-handed, even though the incidence of left-handedness is greater among them than among most other people.

It should also be noted in passing that there is nothing about either mathematics or chess that would make them easier to do with one hand rather than the other. Neither is like playing first base, which is intrinsically easier for a left-hander. In short, the higher than average incidence of left-handedness among first basemen can be traced to the nature of the activity itself. But the same is not true for mathematicians or top-rated chess players—or for astronauts, architects and others in occupations and activities requiring high levels of analytical skills, which also have higher than average incidences of left-handedness.[17]

The resources used up in the disproportionate development of one region of the brain may be taken from more than one place and this place may differ from individual to individual. Among the brain functions controlled in the vicinity of the region of the brain controlling analytical thinking is speech.[18] In Einstein's brain, his unusually large region controlling analytical and spatial reasoning spread over into nearby areas of the brain, normally used for other functions—including speech.

Neuroscientists who have noted that Einstein's brain was extraordinarily developed in a region associated with mathematical and spatial reasoning have also noted that there are "adjacent areas involved in language," which seem to have gotten less than their usual development in his brain.[19] What is not known is whether that is why he talked late. The facts, however, are sufficiently striking to have caused some neuroscientists to suggest the possibility of a connection.[20] As Professor Steven Pinker of M.I.T. put it:

> The neuroscientists speculated that Einstein's parietal lobes expanded early in prenatal development, giving him larger, undivided lobules that accommodated richer and more tightly integrated circuits for mathematical and spatial reasoning. This may help explain Einstein's other famous cognitive trait: he did not speak until he was 3 years old. Many late-talking children grow up

to be engineers, mathematicians, and scientists, including the physicists Richard Feynman and Edward Teller. Perhaps this is because different mental functions compete for brain real estate as they develop in the cerebral cortex.[21]

If these neuroscientists are right and Einstein's brain began to form in this unusual way before he was born, and even if something similar happened to many or most of the children in the two groups studied here, that still leaves many other children whose late talking may have nothing whatever to do with any such brain development patterns.

Late-Talking Children

Although we tend to think of the children in the groups studied here as youngsters who talk late *despite* their precocious development in analytical thinking, it is also possible that they talk late *because* of their precocious development in analytical thinking.

Since the entire brain grows in early childhood, producing more total resources that can then be used for various functions, this hypothesis is consistent with the fact that bright, late-talking children do eventually begin to speak and that their speech development usually catches up with that of other children in a few years.

What is also consistent with this hypothesis is the futility of many efforts to get them to talk during their earlier years, when other children are talking, and their later spontaneous—sometimes sudden—development of speech without any additional efforts by adults. Indeed, the child may begin to speak after the adults have given up hope and stopped making any efforts. Noted language authority and neuroscientist Steven Pinker of M.I.T. says, "language seems to develop about as quickly as the growing brain can handle it."[22] While this was a statement about the general development of language, it may be especially relevant to bright children who talk late.

What is also consistent with this hypothesis is the sudden speeding up of speech development, as in the case of a girl whose vocabulary roughly doubled in her 40th month and then doubled again in her 41st month, with her speech also becoming more sophisticated in the process.[23] In the absence of any special efforts by adults during those two months, such results seem much more consistent with brain development than with external causes. Moreover, this was not an isolated case. A number of silent children have suddenly and spontaneously begun speaking in complete sentences, as Edward Teller did.

Yet another fact consistent with this hypothesis is that many bright children who have not yet begun talking have no difficulty understanding what other people are saying to them and may even follow complex instructions better than most other children their age. In this respect, they may be like Leslie in Chapter 2, who was late in talking but who scored at the 99th percentile in her comprehension of words.[24] Since understanding what others are saying is usually a function of the *right* hemisphere of the brain, while the production of speech is usually a function of the left hemisphere, extraordinary development of analytical functions in the left hemisphere might risk adversely affecting the ability to speak without affecting the ability to comprehend speech. As the author who studied Leslie put it:

> She learned melodies easily, learned intonation patterns easily, and mimicked nonspeech sounds . . . While language is primarily localized in the left hemisphere of the brain, the learning of melodies and intonation contours is located in the right hemisphere.[25]

Differences between the sexes in the organization and functioning of the brain may help explain why the great majority of bright children who talk late are boys. The greater specialization within the male brain leaves each function more vulnerable to disruption than in the female brain, which can often do the same thing in more places. Thus a lack of resources in one particular region of the brain may be less likely to stop a girl from developing speech, when her brain is more capable of performing the same function elsewhere. These are of course all generalizations, since individual brains differ in their organization. As we have already seen, those few bright girls who talk late tend to have other individual and family characteristics very similar to those of bright boys who talk late.

Because today's parents, as contrasted with parents of a generation or so ago, are unlikely to leave a late-talking child alone to develop on his own, it may not be possible to know whether a given child learned to talk because of speech therapy or because of his or her own natural brain development. What is known is that many similar children in previous generations began to talk on their own before "early intervention" programs became widespread. How many children then and how many now remains unknown.

While we need to be clear that we are considering an hypothesis, we also need to be clear that it is not simply a theory out of thin air. There is solid empirical research behind the location of certain functions in the brain and about differences in the organization and functioning of male and female brains. There is also hard evidence on the incidence of left-handedness among people in various professions,[26] as well as the incidences of allergies and myopia among high-IQ people in general. Empirical research has also shown that very young children tend to recover better than adults from localized brain damage in the region of the left hemisphere which normally controls speech,[27] suggesting that local specialization within the brain has not yet gone as far as it does in adults.

What remains to be examined scientifically by specialists is how all this fits together. Children talk late for so many different reasons and have so many different collateral characteristics that it will be a challenge for the future—and for others—to untangle all the complex factors at work. Here we are seeking only to grope toward some understanding of why one particular subset of children with highly developed analytical and other mental abilities are also years late in beginning to speak. Because these children so often come from families where close relatives are concentrated in highly analytical and musical occupations, heredity seems like a promising factor to investigate. Though we are far from a scientific answer, the relevant questions seem more likely to revolve around the hereditary characteristics of the brain and its development than the usual explanations based on blaming parents—especially mothers—for the way they raised the child. In most families with a bright child who talked late, the other children did not talk late, even though raised by the same parents.[28] In some of these families—including my own—the late-talking child had a sibling who talked early. Such differences are much easier to reconcile with normal genetic variations ("Mendelian variations") than with parenting practices.[29] Nor is it a matter of the parents' making mistakes with the late-talking child that were not repeated with later children. The children in my group were sometimes the oldest, sometimes the youngest, and often in between.

Questions about the relative influences of heredity and environment do not necessarily have one answer for all children. While variations in childhood language development in the general population seem to reflect both heredity and environment, with the latter being the predominant influence, nevertheless for those children who are in the bottom 5 percent verbally at age two, heredity seems to play the predominant role, according to a British study of thousands of two-year-olds. Nor are these children in the bottom 5 percent simply retarded across the board. While 22 percent of the children in this bottom group had non-verbal delays in development as well, most did not.

In short, when a child is lagging far behind in speech development at age two, the reason is far more likely to be heredity than environment and, in most cases, it is not due to any apparent general retardation. As the authors of the British study point out: "We know from longitudinal studies that many children with language delays at two do prove to be 'late bloomers' who subsequently catch up with their peers."[30] In other words, if delayed speech at age two is considered a disorder, this study suggests that it is usually *not* part of a pervasive pattern, despite the apparent popularity of the phrase "pervasive developmental disorder" among too many people diagnosing late-talking children.

Williams Syndrome

Further evidence that a disproportionate share of the brain's resources going to one function can leave other functions impaired can be found in another group of children, those with "Williams syndrome," whose characteristics are almost directly the opposite of those of children with the Einstein syndrome. In the Williams syndrome children, a part of the brain associated with language and sociability has been found to be unusually enlarged, leading to children like this:

> Kristen Aerts is only 9 years old, but she can work a room like a seasoned pol. She marches into the lab of cognitive neuroscientist Ursala Bellugi . . . and greets her with a cheery, "Good morning, Dr. Bellugi. How are you today?" The youngster smiles at a visitor and says, "My name is Kristen. What's yours?" She looks people in the

eye when she speaks and asks questions—social skills that many adults never seem to master, much less a third grader.[31]

Yet, despite such precocious poise and social adroitness, Kristen cannot write her own address and has trouble subtracting 2 from 4 or tying her own shoes. She has a low IQ and may never be able to live independently. This is typical of children with Williams syndrome. They have all the things that bright children who talk late seem to lack in childhood and lack all the things in which our late-talkers excel. While children with the Einstein syndrome excel at putting puzzles together and many learn to read early, children with Williams syndrome have trouble with puzzles and many of them never develop the ability to read beyond the first-grade level. Yet, in verbal communication, children with the Williams syndrome can understand complex sentences and can correct sentences that have grammatical mistakes.[32]

In addition to their ability to understand words and grammar, such children "have the gift of gab, telling elaborate stories with unabashed verve and incorporating audience teasers, such as 'Gadzooks!' and 'Lo and behold!'"[33] The facility of these children with words is illustrated by a girl named Crystal:

> In describing her future aspirations, Crystal, a 16-year-old adolescent, states: "You're looking at a professional book writer. My books will be filled with drama, action, and excitement. And everyone will want to read them. I'm going to write books, page after page, stack after stack . . . I'll start on Monday." Crystal describes a meal as "a sumptuous buffet," an older friend as "quite elegant," and her boyfriend as "my sweet petunia"; when asked if someone could borrow her watch, she replies "My watch is always available for service." Crystal can spontaneously create original stories —she weaves a tale of a chocolate princess who changes the sun color to save the

chocolate world from melting; she recounts with detail a dream in which an alien from a different planet emerges from a television. Her creativity extends to music; she has composed the lyrics of a love song.

In view of her facility with language, proclivity for flowery, descriptive terms, and professed focus on drama and action, her aspiration may seem plausible; but in fact, Crystal has an IQ of 49 . . . has reading, writing and math skills comparable to those of a first or second grader, demonstrates visuospatial abilities of a 5-year-old, and requires a babysitter for supervision.[34]

"What makes Williams syndrome so fascinating," says Dr. Ursula Bellugi, "is it shows that the domains of cognition and language are quite separate."[35] That principle is also illustrated by the very different children in our studies, those with the Einstein syndrome. The latter can outgrow their problems, while the former are handicapped for life.

The fact that a disproportionate development of one part of the brain is recognized as the reason for the set of characteristics called the Williams syndrome makes it not unreasonable to consider the possibility that the opposite set of characteristics in children with the Einstein syndrome may also be due to a disproportionate development of another part of the brain.

Idiot Savants

If children with Williams syndrome are located at one end of a spectrum and children with the Einstein syndrome are located toward the other end of the spectrum, then people with a more usual mix of various skills—"normal" people—would be located in the region between them. Even farther out beyond those with the

Einstein syndrome would be people capable of extraordinary feats of the mind in very narrow areas, but so incapable of even ordinary intellectual perception otherwise that they have been called "idiot savants" in the past and today simply "savants." The older description captures the paradox of such people, while the later usage sacrifices accuracy for the sake of sensitivity or politeness.

There are, for example, some mentally retarded or autistic children who learn to play a musical instrument—usually a piano—at a very young age and other young children who can draw almost photographic pictures of a scene before them or who can sketch remarkable drawings from memory.

All of the artists like this have been autistic. One such artist in Britain, Stephen Wiltshire, was diagnosed with infantile autism as a toddler and in later years had his drawings published when he was thirteen years old. A teacher of his described "this little boy, who sat on his own in a corner of the room, drawing."

> Stephen used to draw and draw and draw and draw—the school called him "the drawer." And they were the most unchildlike drawings, like St. Paul's and Tower Bridge and other London landmarks in tremendous detail, when other children his age were just drawing stick figures. It was the sophistication of his drawings, their mastery of line and perspective, that amazed me—and these were all there when he was seven.[36]

Yet Stephen could not even cross a street by himself nor maintain a serious conversation with anyone.[37]

A musical idiot-savant who became famous in the American antebellum South was a young black slave boy known as Blind Tom. His musical talent was discovered accidentally, as a result of his having overheard piano lessons being given to his owner's daughters:

> Colonel Bethune ... heard piano playing late at night and went down to investigate, where he found the four-year-old Tom playing without a mistake a Mozart sonata that he had heard the Bethune daughters practicing.[38]

By the age of eight, Blind Tom was giving concerts locally and, two years later, began giving concerts throughout the South.[39] Eventually his renown became such that he was invited to the White House, where he played the piano for President James Buchanan. Yet indications are that Blind Tom was mentally retarded or autistic, though autism as a concept would not emerge until the next century. A contemporary simply described him as having "but little of human nature."[40] Before his musical talents were accidentally discovered, Blind Tom was just a little boy who sat off in a corner by himself.

An autistic musical prodigy of our times, who has also become a world-class chess player, is an Australian of Chinese ancestry named Trevor Tao. In 1989, at the age of eleven, he played Dvorak's "New World Symphony" on a piano, without a note of music in front of him.[41]

Incidentally, one of his brothers received a Ph.D. in mathematics from Princeton at age 19 and went on to become a professor of mathematics at UCLA.

While Trevor Tao has shown signs of unusually high intelligence, especially in mathematics, there have been many other musical prodigies who were mentally retarded. Astonishingly, a majority of these retarded or autistic musical prodigies have been either congenitally blind or severely visually impaired.[42]

It is remarkable enough that so many of them have been blind, but what is directly relevant to the hypothesis being considered here is that it is *congenital* blindness, as distinguished from blindness that might occur later on, as a result of injury or disease. Blindness that develops in adulthood may leave the optical system of the brain useless, but the resources specialized for use in the optical system may not be as readily available for other uses as they might be in an infant, whose brain resources had not yet become so specialized to particular functions. At that early stage of life, unused resources in the brain are subject to what specialists call "rededication" to other uses.

In short, the high incidence of congenital blindness among musical savants raises the question whether differences in the allocation of brain resources may not be involved here, as in other anomalies. Unused resources normally employed for one function, such as sight, may be available to allow extraordinary development of some other function. The theory of a "rededication" of brain resources in early life has been used in other contexts involving idiot savants,[43] so it is not a very original idea here to suggest that the same thing might apply to blind musical savants.

This possibility would not imply that all congenitally blind and mentally deficient children would become musical prodigies. But the extraordinarily high incidence of blindness among retarded and autistic musical prodigies suggests that "rededication" of brain resources might be an enabling condition, even if it is not a sufficient condition by itself.

Being a musical prodigy involves much more than manual dexterity with particular instruments. It involves a keener perception of pitch and other musical characteristics than most people have, as well as perhaps more appreciation of the emotional depths of the music. Even autistic children have been known to respond emotionally to music.[44] While what is called "perfect pitch" or "absolute pitch" is found in only about one out of ten thousand adults, it is much more common among musical savants.[45] As already noted, perfect pitch has been linked to special brain characteristics. Hearing is not just a matter of the ears, but also of the brain's processing of what comes in from the ears—and some brains can do this much more finely than others.

There have been other idiot savants in other fields. For example:

> The story of Alonzo Clemmons, a severely retarded young black man, has appeared on both national television and in *The New York Times*. Alonzo produces extraordinarily beautiful sculptures, primarily of animals. His skill in sculpting was discovered only when a worker at the institution where he resided chanced upon Alonzo's collection of tiny sculptures of various animals, composed of tar he had dug from the parking lot with his fingernails! His exceptional talent was quickly recognized, and bronze copies of his works now sell in art galleries for thousands of dollars.[46]

The theory of "rededication" of brain resources in early life has been applied to artistic savants, as well as musical savants. As Bernard Rimland, a noted authority on autism, and Deborah Fein, a neuropsychologist, have put it:

> Normal children find intrinsically interesting the faces and voices of other people and pay them much attention in the early months and years of life. Perhaps a primary motivational abnormality, that of social disinterest, leads the autistic child at an early age to disregard the faces and speech of other people. The language-comprehension (left temporal) and face-recognition (bilateral intertemporal) cortical areas may need a wide and varied base of input in early life in order to develop their highly specialized mechanisms for comprehension and recognition. In the motivally based absence of such input, such areas may not be strongly dedicated to these functions and may thus be available to serve the higher but nonsocial pattern-recognition functions of the auditory and visual systems that they, respectively, adjoin.[47]

In support of this theory, they point to two famous autistic artists who "appear to have a marvelous sense of color and/or form, but both are remarkable for their inept representations of the human face."[48] By contrast, children with Williams syndrome "exhibit a remarkable ability in processing, discriminating, and remembering faces."[49]

These and other mentally retarded or autistic prodigies give glimpses of some of the incredible things that the human brain is capable of—but which it may not be capable of doing simultaneously with all the other things that it needs to do. As in the case of Einstein, so in the case of the autistic artists mentioned above, the functions that are extraordinarily developed are controlled from regions of the brain located close to regions from which the malfunctioning operations are controlled—again, adding weight to the idea that one function is taking resources that would normally go to a different function. Fortunately, Einstein and other children with a similar development pattern have been able to outgrow these early childhood malfunctions as the brain itself has grown and more resources became available for the neglected function.

Speech Therapists

With all that science has discovered, there remains so much about the brain which no one yet understands that dogmatic pretensions of "expertise" on the part of semi-professional evaluators of children should be warning signs for parents. In an area where no one has "*the* answer," you might think that there would be reticence and caution, along with a desire to learn more. In fact, however, there is not only much haste and dogmatism, but also too often a resistance to learning more, especially from anyone outside the occupational coterie.

A child psychiatrist who is also the mother of a late-talking girl encountered complete disinterest when she tried to discuss recent research findings with a speech-language pathologist whom she interviewed as a possible therapist for her daughter. After working with many other speech-language pathologists as well, this psychiatrist concluded that they were "not very sophisticated in their scientific understanding of child language or speech development." Many of them "are very ignorant of neurologic maturation"—in fact, "so ignorant that they don't even realize how much they don't know."

Another mother recommended *Late-Talking Children* to a speech/language pathologist, with this result: "I felt immediately her resistance to being 'taught' something by a prospective patient's mother, and I felt her condescension when I tried to encapsulate something of the thesis of *Late-Talking Children*." Some good came out of all this, however. Once the mother saw the know-it-all attitude of this speech pathologist, she cancelled an appointment that she had made to have her evaluate her son.

Whatever speech therapists may or may not be able to do for a particular child, they are unlikely to be the most reliable or unbiased source of information as to whether a given child needs speech therapy in the first place. If the reason a particular child is behind schedule in beginning to talk is a matter of brain maturation, then the therapy sessions could be little more than sources of frustration to all concerned before the child's brain has developed to the point of being ready for speech. Some parents have in fact reported such frustrating experiences, which are consistent with Professor Pinker's conclusion that "language seems to develop about as quickly as the growing brain can handle it."[50] On the other hand, there are other considerations when deciding whether or when to have speech therapy. Studies indicate that there is not an unlimited window of opportunity for a child to begin learning to speak. The brain not only grows with the passing years, it also goes through metamorphoses that enable it to do particular things more readily at one period of life than at another.[51] Acquiring the ability to speak is much more easily done in the first half-dozen years of life than later on. For late-talking children, the interval between the window of opportunity opening and its beginning to close may be much shorter than for most other children.

The median age at which the children in Stephen Camarata's group began to speak was three and a half years old and in my group was four. Noted language development authority Steven Pinker of M.I.T. gives age six as the point beyond which the ability to learn to speak for the first time begins to decline, as the brain metamorphoses and adapts itself to new tasks. The ability to acquire language for the first time continues to decline until puberty and becomes "rare thereafter."[52] While it is possible to learn new languages thereafter—though usually not nearly as readily or as well as foreign languages are learned in early childhood—it is grasping the concept of language in general for the first time and mastering its requirements that is the big hurdle. That is what the brain begins losing its ability to do after early childhood.

Between the time when the child is clearly ready to speak and the time when learning to speak becomes more difficult, speech therapy may speed up a process that has already begun. As with so many other things, speech therapy is neither categorically good nor categorically bad. Everything depends on the circumstances, the timing, and the individual child.

In some cases, and especially where late talking is a result of other things besides an unusual brain maturation pattern, the therapist may be able to "jump start" the speech development process. Given the fact that most parents of the late-talkers in my study and in Professor Camarata's study began to be seriously concerned when the child was two years old, merely speeding up the process can bring relief from great parental anxieties, even if the child would have begun to speak later and just as well without it. In addition, the child's own social development may be helped very much by earlier development of the ability to speak, possibly preventing the formation of enduring habits of anti-social withdrawal. In short, there are potentially great benefits from speech therapy, depending on the particular child, the particular therapist, and other circumstances. The benefits seem most likely to outweigh the costs and dangers when the therapist dispenses therapy, rather than attempting to make diagnoses that go beyond what most therapists are trained to understand.

SOCIAL CHARACTERISTICS

Even if this hypothesis about the organization and functioning of the brain should prove to be correct in its applicability to bright children who talk late—and scientific research on its applicability to this subset of children has barely begun—there would still be many ancillary facts to explain. Why are bright children who talk late so often also late in toilet training? Why are they so often described as "strong-willed," to use a term that appears over and over in letters from parents of such children? Why do they tend to be loners, at least during their early years?

While there are as yet no definitive answers, there have been all too many dogmatic pronouncements, often coming from people not qualified to make any diagnosis, but equipped with an arsenal of jargon and a readiness to pronounce parents to be "in denial" when they resist sweeping labels and the programs toward which they are being pushed.

Autism is one of the labels often used, in part because it is in vogue and in part because it brings in more government money than a label of delayed speech. Another fashionable label is "hyperlexia."

Among the defining symptoms of hyperlexia is that hyperlexic children "may have exceedingly long attention spans, but only for activities of their own choosing."[53] Otherwise, it may be that the child "flits from one activity to another without ever completing anything."[54] In other words, behavior that is common among high-IQ children in general is treated as a dangerous symptom when a particular child's behavior is put under a microscope because of some other deviation from the norm, whether that is talking late or reading early.

Ironically, a child may be regarded as having "rigid thinking"—one of the hallmarks of autism—when it is precisely the adults who are rigid in their thinking. For example, one late-talking little girl was told to "dab" when painting and instead she chose to stroke. When her mother was told that this was an example of "rigid thinking," she replied: "Yeah, on the teacher's part!" Unfortunately, too few parents are willing to contradict the "experts" like this. Teachers' rigid insistence that children sit in a circle has caused many needless clashes, not to mention dire conclusions about the child who does not go along.

It is not enough to compare the social characteristics of children. The age at which these characteristics exist is also important. We have seen in the first two chapters that the social development of children with Einstein's syndrome may lag far behind that of their peers in early childhood—and yet the late-talkers may have a normal distribution of social characteristics as adults, some even working in fields requiring considerable social skills, such as the media and politics, while others tend to remain shy in adulthood and may specialize in fields such as engineering, where social skills are not crucial.

While some of these characteristics may overlap with characteristics found among autistic children, children with Asperger Syndrome, or with high-IQ children, there are also important differences that are often overlooked by those who are quick to label. For example, the unsociable characteristics of bright children who talk late do not generally seem to persist into adulthood, as they do with even highly intelligent autistic children. Some high-ability autistic individuals who have gone on to successful careers —Temple Grandin, a Ph.D., being perhaps the best known— nevertheless remain socially far behind their peers as adults.[55] The pattern found among children with the Einstein syndrome is more similar to the pattern found among children with very high IQs in general—more social maladjustments in childhood than in adulthood.[56]

Although some bright children who talk late have been diagnosed as having Asperger's Syndrome—a variant of, or related to, autism—children with Asperger's Syndrome do not talk late. Professor Camarata at Vanderbilt has emphatically informed parents of late-talking children that any diagnoses of their children as having Asperger's Syndrome are just plain wrong.[57] There is overlap in the two sets of children's abilities and interests in analytical thinking, but there is also contrast when it comes to speaking.

As for children with very high IQs in general, we have already seen that some of their characteristics—concentration, solitary work or play, marching to their own drummer—also overlap with those of the children with the Einstein Syndrome. However, seldom is such overlap noted in either scholarly discussion or clinical diagnosis. The children studied here also overlap with autistic children in having a disproportionate number of engineers among their parents and grandparents.[58] But these and other overlaps by themselves are not conclusive, though too often they may be treated as if they were. The variety of overlaps among different kinds of children makes a mechanical checklist approach dangerous as a basis for diagnosis or treatment.

The emotional and social development of autistic adults has often been characterized as "childlike"—which is to say, a set of characteristics that might be considered normal in young children. Similarly, the inability of children with Williams syndrome to read beyond a first-grade level would not be unusual among children who were in fact in the first grade. In other words, the particular stage of life at which an individual has certain social characteristics is as significant as the characteristics themselves.

A study of children with hyperlexia, who share some of the characteristics of the children in the groups studied by Professor Camarata and me, found that at ages two or three such children display many of the characteristics of autistic children and "appear to be autistic." However, "when language comprehension and expression improve, the autistic behaviors diminish or disappear."[59]

Unfortunately, the checklist approach to evaluation can find many unusual characteristics in young children that might be fraught with implications if these characteristics continued on into later life, but which may represent simply passing stages otherwise. This can be especially so with children whose speech is delayed, creating a host of problems in social interactions and emotional pressures—but problems which can fade away with the development of the ability to talk. Again, it cannot simply be *assumed* that this will happen automatically with any given child, but neither should the results of a checklist be assumed to be set in stone.

THE EINSTEIN SYNDROME

Using the term "the Einstein syndrome" does not of course imply that a bright child who talks late is going to grow up to become another Albert Einstein. There may never be another Einstein. The Einstein syndrome is simply a convenient label for unusually bright children with delayed speech development. However, these children often share enough other characteristics that they are in fact a special phenomenon. To summarize these characteristics:

1. Outstanding and precocious analytical abilities and/or musical abilities
2. Outstanding memories
3. Strong wills
4. Highly selective interests, leading to unusual achievements in some areas and disinterest and ineptness in others
5. Delayed toilet training
6. Precocious ability to read and/or use numbers and/or use computers
7. Close relatives in occupations requiring outstanding analytical and/or musical abilities
8. Unusual concentration and absorption in what they are doing

Other characteristics, not studied systematically or found pervasively, have occurred often enough to be notable—extreme reactions to ordinary stimuli, including ferocious tantrums as small children, being "loners" among their peers, and often being alienated from school and/or encountering negative reactions from teachers. These latter problems in institutional settings often begin in kindergarten or nursery school and continue on for years, long past the time when these children are speaking normally. Indeed, similar patterns of extreme sensitivity and strong reactions to ordinary stimuli, loneliness, and alienation from peers and teachers, have been found among high-IQ children in general,[60] most of whom do not talk late.

Because such children are so often misunderstood, parents cannot let themselves be rushed or intimidated into programs that can be counterproductive for their son or daughter. Still more should they resist the use of drugs, without getting independent medical advice from people who have no connection whatever with existing programs that need a continuing supply of children to justify their existence.

Multiple independent opinions are a layman's only protection from the biases or idiosyncrasies of a particular professional. Those professionals who refuse to make an independent assessment without knowing what previous assessments have been should be left alone, even if that means going to another community or another state to get another evaluation. The stakes are just too high to let adults' turf and ego considerations determine a child's future. For those parents who find it impossible to get a professional evaluation from someone who does not insist on seeing what others have said, it may be worth a trip to Vanderbilt University to see Professor Stephen Camarata, who does not require knowing what others have said before making his own evaluation. As an alternative, he may be able to recommend professionals he knows in the parents' vicinity who will be willing to make wholly independent evaluations.

It is well worth the extra effort to get a good second opinion. Reliable diagnoses are hard to find—and unreliable diagnoses are usually no farther away than your local school district. While these school district evaluations are free, they can be the most costly "free" thing of your life—and your child's life.

SUMMARY AND IMPLICATIONS

While no one knows specifically or with certainty why some very bright children talk late, what is known is that there are other brain-related abnormalities that are more common among very bright people than in the general population. Children with the Einstein syndrome are not unique in that respect, however puzzling they may seem to their parents or to those who come in contact with them in medical or educational institutions. Explanations offered by researchers who have studied other brain-related disorders among very bright people—that a disproportionate share of the brain's resources going to intellectual functions can leave inadequate resources for some other brain functions—may apply to bright children who talk late, as well as to bright people with higher incidences of allergies, myopia, and left-handedness.

Both the statistical patterns among bright children who talk late and their personal and family histories are more compatible with this explanation than with such alternative explanations as the parents' child-rearing practices. So is the imperviousness of many of these children to attempts to get them to talk at the ages when other children talk—and their later spontaneous development of speech as their brains grow with the rest of their bodies. So is the fact that the overwhelming majority of children with the Einstein syndrome are boys, given that the organization of the male brain makes it more vulnerable to localized problems. The fact that an opposite set of characteristics among children with Williams syndrome has already been found to be due to a disproportionate development of particular regions of their brains adds weight to this explanation of children with the Einstein syndrome.

While this explanation does not, by itself, account for such related phenomena as strong wills and strong preoccupations and aversions, such patterns have been found among high IQ individuals in general, most of whom do not talk late. In short, all this seems to go with the intellectual territory, even if we do not yet know why.

Unfortunately, this explanation is not compatible with the interests and beliefs of many speech therapists, special education teachers, and others who press parents toward the use of their services. The difficulty of separating out children with the Einstein syndrome from many other children who talk late for many other reasons also means that honest mistakes can be common, especially among semi-professionals relying on superficial checklists, preconceptions, and jargon. Add to this mixture anxious or even desperate parents, and there are all the ingredients of much needless anguish for families and much misdirection of children into programs that can do lasting damage, as well as leaving lasting labels to follow a child for years afterwards. Coping with such problems in an atmosphere of uncertainty is the challenge addressed in the next two chapters.

Chapter 5

Tests and Evaluations

Whatever the reasons that may ultimately become known as to why some very bright children are late in talking, any given parent's problem is what to do here and now. There is certainly no lack of options. The great number of very different options is in fact one of the problems. Nor is there any shortage of people and programs offering everything from a dim hope to miracle cures. These people and these programs can also be a big part of the problem.

Merely getting an accurate evaluation can be a considerable challenge. So can seeking a second opinion that is *independent* of the first opinion—without which it is not really a second opinion. The labels that result from these evaluations are yet another problem, not only as regards their meaning or accuracy, but also as regards how indelible these labels may be, following the child for years, regardless of how well-founded or how ill-founded that label may have been originally or how much has changed as the child's development has unfolded.

The question as to whether to have "early intervention" or to let the child develop at his own pace is also a dilemma, with potentially serious consequences, no matter which choice is made. Then there is the question as to whether the child's social development will be helped or hindered by putting him into some form of institutional day care. None of these choices is as easy as they may be made to seem by those with a vested interest in serving their own agenda, rather than the best interests of your child.

No responsible parent can simply do nothing and hope for the best when a child is late in learning to speak. Professional evaluations are essential, but no single evaluation should be taken as gospel. This is an area where even scholars and scientists have only limited knowledge, and where many practitioners are often mistaken in their diagnosis and treatment. Some professionals, and especially semi-professionals like social workers and school personnel, have airs of "expertise" and an arsenal of jargon and dogmas, but no one knows exactly why some very bright children talk late.

What can be done is to have the child checked for medical problems and for mental deficiencies—and then get multiple diagnoses that are independent of one another and also independent of any treatment program that needs a continuing supply of children to treat. A physician's examination and some non-verbal mental tests are a necessary beginning, though only a beginning.

It might seem obvious that any mental test for a child with verbal problems should be non-verbal, in order to see if he has problems other than the one already known. Yet many such children are given verbal tests. Other obviously inappropriate tests may be given to other kinds of children. One child in my group who is legally blind was given a test which included questions that required normal eyesight. Although his IQ score on this particular test placed him in the mentally retarded range, his IQ on a different test placed him in the above-normal range. Nor was he the only child whose

IQ score has gone from an apparently mentally retarded level to a level above the national average, just from a change of IQ test.

Parents should never simply *assume* reasonableness on the part of evaluators, when a bureaucratic routine can lead to disastrous conclusions and counterproductive actions based on those conclusions. Insist on a non-verbal mental test. Your child's future is more important than the huffiness or condescension of those who wrap themselves in the mantle of their own "professional" status or "expertise."

Although Professor Stephen Camarata is an authority on childhood language disorders, he nevertheless has the children who come to his clinic checked first by a physician. This is a precaution that parents would do well to emulate. If no physical or mental defects turn up—as has been the case with many of the children in the groups studied by Professor Camarata and myself—then other causes might be evaluated and various courses of action considered.

How often are the diagnoses wrong and by how much? According to Helen Tager-Flusberg, a professor of neurosciences at the University of Massachusetts:

> I am in pretty regular contact with families who have children with a range of neurodevelopmental disorders, including autism spectrum disorders . . . Almost all are completely frustrated with their interactions with their educational institutions and don't feel that the evaluations of school personnel have much validity. Their experiences with other professionals is mixed—most are fairly positive but there are the regular stories we hear about misdiagnoses, etc. I would say that at least ¾ of the histories I read include at least one report that is completely off the mark.

Even though a case history may contain more than one evaluation, it is still chilling to think that three-quarters of the case histories contain at least one evaluation that is "completely off the mark." Perhaps even more chilling was a *defense* of inaccurate diagnoses by a speech therapist who claimed that families coped better when they had a label for their child's late talking—even if that label was autism—rather than simply calling it "a speech language delay of unknown origin" because "the 'demon' loses its power" once it is named.

> We may not really know WHAT this set of behaviors means, but the closest NAMED disorder with that set of behaviors is X . . . let's call it that, and then move on to provide a supportive linguistic environment to encourage communication. We may discover through this remediation process that we were WRONG about the initial SUSPECTED label. Which is cool, as long as we are continuously EVALUATING PROGRESS AND METHODS SO THAT WE KNOW AND WILL ADMIT IT.

This blithely ignores the enormous and lasting anguish needlessly inflicted on desperate and trusting parents. Moreover, the "services" provided may not always be as important or effective as this therapist assumes—and some are counterproductive. As a psychiatrist who is also the mother of a late-talking child said in a letter to me, "it is hard to tell whether progress is simply because the child is getting older or because of the speech therapy, when both are happening at the same time." In some special education programs, a child whose only problem is delayed speech development is put in classes with children with much more severe mental and behavioral problems. This can have not only negative effects on the child's morale and mental development, it can also lead to imitation of other children's misbehavior, both at school and at home.

Speech therapists sometimes depict themselves as experts whose understanding supersedes that of medical doctors specializing in the general treatment of children. Where pediatricians find nothing physically or mentally wrong with a child, their advice is often just to wait for the child's natural speech development to take its course—as they may well have seen happen many times before. A typical response of a speech therapist to such advice is that pediatricians "are not trained speech therapists" and concerns about a child's language development should be taken to "the specialist trained in this area, a speech-language pathologist."[1] This might make sense if the issue were simply *who* should provide therapy to the child. But, when the issue is *whether* a given child needs therapy in the first place, then the pediatrician's training and experience may be more reliable, as well as less biased by self-interest, since pediatricians are unlikely to administer speech therapy themselves.

In some cases, a speech therapist's services may be very useful in treatment, but speech therapists are seldom qualified to diagnose autism or other conditions that they too often attempt to diagnose. In short, speech therapists are most valuable when engaged in speech therapy and most dangerous when engaged in diagnosis. A parent who remains worried after a pediatrician's diagnosis might get a second medical opinion from a neurologist or a child psychiatrist, or perhaps another pediatrician. But a diagnosis that can affect the course of a child's life is too serious to be left solely in the hands of speech therapists, social workers or other semi-professionals. Speech-language pathologists with Ph.D.s, such as Professor Camarata at Vanderbilt, are another story. But here we are talking about the ordinary, garden-variety semi-professionals that parents are likely to encounter in local school districts and the like.

Semi-professionals have produced some truly appalling evaluations of young children who are late in talking. For example, one report says, "Aaron is emerging into the locutionary stage of intentionality." In other words, he is starting to talk. At the end of several more pages of such stilted language to describe ordinary things, there is a brief paragraph of conclusions stating that the child's characteristics "are consistent with the characteristics of autism, therefore this diagnosis has been made." This non-sequitur is signed by five people, none of them with a medical degree or a Ph.D. Most of the characteristics of a Chevrolet "are consistent with the characteristics" of a Rolls Royce, but no one concludes that a Chevy is therefore a Rolls. Yet such sloppy reasoning is allowed to put an indelible label on a child and shape his future, quite aside from the needless pain that parents are often put through by a false diagnosis.

The dangers of a mechanical checklist approach come from the fact that many items on a checklist may apply to very different people and very different conditions. Mice and giraffes each have four legs, a tail, fur, two ears, a digestive tract, and many other things in common. Yet we have no trouble telling them apart because we also take notice of the ways in which they are different. But checklists of "symptoms" are not always accompanied by a checklist of differences. Nor are the people who use these checklists always sufficiently trained or sophisticated to see the need for such a precaution.

The superficiality of some of these checklists would have to be seen to be believed. For example, one checklist used for evaluating small children has 15 pages of short items such as "separates easily from parent," "asks for adult help when needed," "shows anticipatory excitement," and "shows positive attitude toward school." The therapist is supposed to assign various points to each of these items and the total number of points at the end of 15 pages is supposed to help diagnose the problem of the child and perhaps change the course of his life for years ahead.

Expressing such guesswork in numbers or pretentious language adds nothing to its validity, though this may be effective in impressing or intimidating some parents. Nor are some specialists in this field above pressuring parents by declaring them to be "in denial" if they do not go along, or by claiming that dire consequences are likely if the child is not put into some treatment program that they are pushing. One mother said: "It was like being pursued by a cult!"

Some parents are of course more susceptible to such tactics than others, and fathers and mothers of the same child may differ in their responses. One of the most dramatic examples of this difference occurred when some school-supplied evaluator pronounced a late-talking little boy "mentally retarded." The mother burst into tears and the father burst into laughter. In this case, the father was Professor Stephen Camarata, who realized from his own professional experience how incompetent the evaluator was.

In another case, both parents refused to believe that their son had "pervasive developmental disorder," despite attempts to "help us out of our 'denial,'" as the mother put it. This father was a psychiatrist and, as the mother said: "My husband has probably seen more true PDD in his practice than any of the health care providers we saw." Most parents have no such expertise to draw on and so are far more vulnerable.

Again and again, not only in our original group but also among other parents who have written to me, the experience has been that school personnel have been among those most ready to label a child "autistic." Autism itself is much rarer than such diagnoses. Studies indicate that from 4 to 10 children out of every 10,000 are autistic.[2] In other words, at most one-tenth of one percent. Yet the label is applied with almost reckless abandon by some, especially by those with no credentials for making any evaluation, such as are too often found in public school systems. A typical letter from a parent who had read *Late-Talking Children* said:

> All of the professionals we have consulted are baffled. How could such an intelligent child have such a large vocabulary of nouns yet have difficulty stringing words together into phrases and sentences?

Those consulted include our pediatrician, a developmental pediatrician at Emory University, a psychiatrist, the head of a communication disorders department at a university in Texas, the Center for Speech and Language Disorders in Chicago, and three independent speech therapists. Interestingly, only the public school system here suggested autism or pervasive development disorder. The professionals, in fact, were outraged at the school system's desire to place Douglas in an autism class.

These parents were wise, not only to get professional advice from outside the school system, but also to get multiple medical and other advice from a variety of independent professional sources before making decisions that could affect the whole future course of their child's life.

The mother of a late-talking four-year-old boy said:

I now believe that the whole procedure of being evaluated is intensely counter-productive with Nicky. Not only does he not "perform" up to his capacity, he performs well below. He withdraws and regresses. I knew this already because at preschool they reported that he didn't know his abc's when he had been happily saying his alphabet and doing alphabet puzzles, etc. at home for at least a year. He isn't classically shy in behavior, but he is wary with strangers, slow to relax, and has an at-home self which is markedly different from his out-in-the-world self.

This child's unwillingness to perform on cue is something that many parents of other late-talking children have noticed and which I recall as well from my son's early years. As one mother put it: "He is not a trained seal." Yet one of the widely used diagnostic checklists has an item that says, "Tell child to: Give block to mommie; put block on table; put block on floor." A cryptic note next to this item says, "pass 2 of 3." But many of the children studied—and others like them—may not choose to do any of these things. Unfortunately, too many testers and therapists regard the fact that a child does not do something as proof that he *cannot* do it. In some cases, the child has been given some very simple task to perform and has chosen instead to do something more complicated and more interesting with the materials provided to him—often leading to a conclusion that he is incapable of the simpler task. Nicky's mother also made some other observations that not only apply to other late-talking children but may have some implications for their behavior in general:

> He also has a kind of dignity and pride which I believe is injured when he senses that he may not succeed at something. It may have something to do with a kind of perfectionism, an acute awareness of his inability to reach his own standards. When he first started drawing circles and lines, they had to be perfect, or he would get frustrated and run away. Instead of allowing himself to experiment and fail, he waits until he can do a task at a high level. This is of course limiting, and we must gently work to overcome it, but he does often perform tasks at a high level once he is willing to perform them at all. For example, he has never colored outside the lines as most children do when they start coloring.

Children with the set of characteristics that we have called the Einstein syndrome may not only fail to do things that they are capable of doing, they may also fail to "understand" things that other children seem to understand—precisely because, like Nicky, they do not like to operate on a superficial or shaky level of understanding.[3] When children seem not to understand things that other children their age seem to understand, a distinction must be made between their not understanding as well as others do and their having higher standards for what it means to understand. This may be a difficult distinction to make in practice, but it will be impossible to make unless the distinction is first recognized in principle when evaluating children in ways that go beyond mechanical checklists.

Having higher standards may be part of the reason why some children remain silent until they are ready to talk in complete sentences. Some other children's higher standards may take other forms. As noted in Chapter 3, a grandfather whose grandson was not yet speaking to anyone overheard the little boy saying words to himself in the back yard when he thought that he was alone. Leslie was likewise observed "furtively rehearsing the word *vanilla*" until finally she said: "Mom, listen to me. I got a vanilla bar."[4]

The mother of a three-year-old girl reported on the Internet:

> We had the second evaluation today and it went better than the first
> . . . She still would not talk to the pathologist, but she would point
> to pictures, so she thinks her receptive language is okay. She did let
> her play with some toys at the end and Renae came alive! She said,
> "look, Mommy, red airplane!" and she started flying it around the
> room. I think this helped the pathologist see that she actually does
> talk, she just does not want to answer stranger's questions!

Although medical people may in general be less dogmatic when dealing with children who are late in talking, hasty judgments are by no means unknown among physicians. Billy's pediatrician, whose dogmatism jeopardized the child's eyesight, was a case in point. Another mother, not part of our group, told of a neurologist who declared her son "mentally retarded" after spending just seven minutes with him, without any physical examination or even touching him, on the basis of the fact that the little boy did not respond to the doctor's questions.

Even an eminent authority can be wrong, as a Canadian mother discovered the hard way:

My son, born in 1983, didn't speak until July or August of 1986. He was three and a half years old. Until then, he had about 4 words, two of which were Mama and Dada. The other two represented water and apple, but sounded nothing like them. The speech delay was only a part of the behaviour that didn't fit the norm.

From the beginning my son, William, was drawn to all things mechanical and electric. He could disassemble and reassemble complicated doorknobs from the age of three. Once, while I was in the basement doing laundry, he removed the basement door knob, removed the bathroom door knob, then installed the bathroom door knob onto the basement door and locked me into the basement. All this in a matter of minutes, and he was three years old. I could fill a very thick book with stories of the things Will did, and I may very well one day. But for now, suffice it to say that he was certainly a going concern.

Doctors in Victoria, British Columbia, Canada first tested William at about age 22 months, and threw out the phrase "mentally retarded". Will attended a special day school there until we moved to our hometown, Montreal, a few months later.

I sought out the finest doctor in Montreal and quite frankly believed I had found him. As a matter of fact, he's been on ABC's 20/20 a couple of times to speak about children's behaviour. This doctor used the word "autistic" on our first visit and so began a nightmare of testing, special schools and therapies.

Will is 16 years old now. He's in advanced mathematics, advanced physics, and has an obvious gift for computer programming and world history. He taught himself to program in grade 5. Just a few days shy of his 16th birthday, he landed a part-time job at Office Depot selling computers. He is by far their youngest employee. He plans to attend University of Waterloo in their computer engineering co-op program. He is funny, witty and loving.

I wish I had been presented with the possibility that he was just very smart when he was a little guy. I believe that the special schools left him with diminished self-esteem that he struggles with to this day. And I struggle with the decisions I made for him at the time. If I could only do it again, I'd leave him be, let him grow and discover and develop in his own sweet time.

By the way, his dad and I met while in engineering school. I was studying to be a civil engineer, his father a mechanical engineer. Neither of us finished, and our lives took very different directions. We were both very strong in mathematics and his father plays classical guitar.

In short, even with physicians, an independent second opinion is essential to guard against the dogmatism of a particular practitioner on something that can affect the course of a child's life. Incidentally, here we see again, in the door knob episode, the analytic bent and interest in assembling and disassembling things that has been common in such children. This analytic bent was expressed by small children, such as Braden and my son John, who figured out child locks, as well as by Richard Feynman and my late-talking college room-mate who could pick regular locks as adults. The enjoyment of assembling things was shown by Kevin and Billy and by young Einstein, among others.

Sometimes it is not professional competence that is lacking in evaluations, but ordinary appreciation of a child's sensitivities. More than one parent has described how some brusque neurologist has practically ripped the child out of the parent's arms and begun undressing him, followed by orders to the distressed child to perform some task. The child's failure to respond under these conditions then became the basis for dire conclusions—all in a matter of minutes.

Even when tests are handled humanely, very bright children often understand that they are considered lacking in some way and develop resentments against the whole testing process. Moreover, testers often read significance into things that would scarcely be noticed in a "normal" child. The mother of a little girl with limited speech had this experience:

> When I told the doctors that Xenia had come to see them for speech delay, they automatically assumed that she was developmentally delayed, autistic, etc. They tested her for hours. She hates tests!! She would cooperate with the doctor for only 10 minutes, and then she would ignore everything he would say. They had to assume that she had a short attention span, because she wouldn't participate more than 10 minutes.
>
> It seems to me that everyone has a microscope looking as diligently as they possibly can to find something wrong with her. The children that are speaking normally are never scrutinized. Whereas when a child does not talk, she is criticized even for the way she walks!

This little girl already skis and does somersaults, but she may well be labelled as someone too uncoordinated to walk properly. Her mother received another glimpse into the way professionals sometimes operate when a speech therapist told her to lie in order to get help that the public schools offer for developmentally delayed children. Specifically, she said that the parents should *not* mention on their application that their daughter skis, dresses herself, knows the alphabet, can spell many words, opens locked doors, uses a computer (including mouse and CD-ROM), plays the piano, and identifies a variety of shapes, such as circles, triangles, octagons, rectangles, etc.

Relatives likewise often assume that a child cannot do whatever he or she does not do. Like professionals who are testing a child, it may never occur to them that the child is bored by the task they are given or are resentful of being tested. When a relative asked this same little girl to point to various items she mentioned on the page of a book, she simply pointed at random to the pictured items. "I could tell that Xenia was not interested because she felt like she was being tested," her mother said later. This relative, however, immediately said, "I think Xenia is retarded" and pointed out that Xenia's cousin the same age did these things faster and better.

This remark was blurted out right in front of the child, as if she were incapable of understanding what was being said. The mother was angry but said nothing. She just began to cry.

Quite aside from the inaccuracies of many evaluations or the pain that these inaccuracies needlessly inflict on parents, the children themselves often become unhappy and resistant to endless evaluations. They can become distressed, angry, or even desperate in evaluation sessions and some develop apprehensions about the simplest medical examination thereafter.

With evaluations, quality is enormously more important than quantity. The "free" evaluations offered by public school districts can be very costly in terms of the psychological trauma inflicted on a young child, not to mention the indelible brand that may follow him for years and the further counterproductive effects of treatments based on misdiagnoses.

The brand may be indelible with the parents themselves, even when a second opinion contradicts the first, as illustrated by one of Professor Camarata's experiences:

> We assessed a child on Monday from Georgia. He was a late talker, but at age five is now in the normal range for expressive and receptive language. His scores are in the low normal range, particularly for comprehension, but definitely in the normal range. His full scale IQ is in the mid 90s, but his academic achievement scores are in the 90th percentile on the Stanford Achievement test (corresponding to

an IQ of approximately 120). The child was labeled autistic at age 3 (he is definitely not autistic). Here's the punch line: In a recent assessment by a psychologist (private practice), the mother was told that her son would never be able to graduate from college. According to the mother, the psychologist said "Look on the bright side, you can now start spending your college fund!" I reviewed the report and see that the psychologist essentially had the same information that we had, but clearly had a different interpretation. I spent a lot of time talking with mom and tried to convince her that IQ is not destiny and that the psychologist's assertions were absurd. Her son has so much potential and the IQ assessment is confounded with verbal skills. What a tragedy!

Some parents seem to think that they should leave no stone unturned. While this is an admirable attitude in some respects, ultimately there is no such thing as certainty. There are only what statisticians call Type I errors and Type II errors—believing that something is true when it is false and believing that something is false when it is true. Not only the probabilities but also the consequences must be weighed—which is why most people do not play Russian roulette. On the other hand, we do not walk around in suits of armor or drive to work in tanks, even though both would add to our security.

Leaving no stone unturned would make sense only if there were no cost to turning stones. In the case of bright children who talk late, these costs can go far beyond the money involved. There can be negative consequences to endless evaluations and unneeded treatment, just as there can be negative consequences to complacency. Perspective is key. Some parents have become alarmed about 18-month-old toddlers who are not yet talking and one mother was concerned when her 9-month old baby was not yet making babbling sounds, as the "norms" said she should be. But every child is not average and even the average child need not be average in everything. Norms are based on statistical averages but averages do not imply that there is no variance.

There is, for example, a whole category of "gifted learning disabled children" on whom articles and books are written— children who are far ahead in some things and far behind in others.[5] The lockstep vision of those who turn "norms" into idols lags hopelessly behind the reality revealed by a growing body of research. These "gifted learning disabled children" are not idiot-savants, but are more like a child named Jane:

> Jane is a 3½-year-old child who is clearly gifted. Her ability for spatial tasks such as assembling blocks to match a model, and replicating complex figures by drawing are extraordinary. Her performance on puzzles and mazes and her visual memory are on a 9-year-old level. While Jane excels in nonverbal skills, her verbal skills are average to poor. She has a problem articulating letters and sounds and her speech is difficult to understand. In trying to make herself understood, Jane becomes easily frustrated. Her ability to express herself is at a 2½-year level. When asked to perform tasks requiring auditory judgment, she will refuse. Jane's receptive language is good, but her productive language is poor. Jane's IQ is in the superior range at 175.[6]

Many learning-disabled/gifted children "are regarded as uncooperative, inattentive, disorganized, tactless, and anti-social." Some parents wonder "why their child, who seemed so bright and alert prior to attending school is suddenly angry and threatens not to go to class."[7] We all need to wonder—if only because the schools themselves are so unlikely to think that they are to blame.

A number of parents report remarkable changes in their children's IQ scores when tested by different people or under different conditions or on different tests. One study described "a learning-disabled boy who scored 89 on a group intelligence test but raised his score to 163 when he was retested on the Stanford-Binet."[8] This enormous change suggests that the principle of a second opinion may be important even in things that are not usually considered to be matters of opinion. When Julia Robinson, later to become a famed mathematician, was given an IQ test in junior high school, she scored 98, two points below normal. One of the mothers in my group reported that her son's IQ was "in the retarded range" when he was four years old but had risen to 115—significantly above-normal—by the time he was ten. Whatever the validity and value of IQ and other mental tests in general, for any particular individual one particular test score should not be regarded as ultimate truth set in stone.

It is not just children who are evaluated. Unofficially, both professionals and lay people such as relatives, neighbors and friends, are often ready to evaluate a child's parents and their home situation. These evaluations are likewise often reckless, including sweeping assumptions by people who know little or nothing about the way a child is raised. For example, an evaluator told Stephen Camarata that the reason his son was not talking was that there was not enough discipline in his home—a home that the evaluator had never seen and one in which there was *more* discipline than in most. A mother was told that her child's delayed speech must be due to not being read to enough—again, a claim made by an evaluator who had no way of knowing how much the child was read to, which was in fact quite a lot.

One of the commonest claims is that parents or siblings of the late-talking child have been so eager to anticipate his wants that he has little incentive to learn to speak. But there is no evidence that this is so. Naturally, when a child is not speaking, his loved ones try to help him, but that does not mean that this help is the cause of the late talking.

Some families in which there are two languages being spoken in the home have been told that it is this confusion of languages which causes the child's delayed speech development. As in other cases, not a speck of evidence is offered to support this theory. Moreover, when such children have finally begun to speak, in cases that have been reported to me, they have spoken and understood both languages. In fact, even before they begin talking, these children have correctly responded to directions given in both languages.

Unfortunately, the recklessness with which conclusions have been reached has not been confined to relatives, neighbors, and friends, but has too often been characteristic of some professionals who should know better.

LABELS

Parents are often justifiably concerned as to whether a label put on their child is accurate—especially since that label can follow the child for years. However, before a label can be either accurate or inaccurate, it must first be meaningful. Too often the labels tell the parents no more than they knew before. For example, one mother wrote that her silent little daughter "has been evaluated by a neurologist who has diagnosed her as having 'a severe communication delay.'" An academic journal offers the following assessment of a group of children whose speech development was behind schedule:

> The common denominator of these children was that they communicate much less than they knew and that they did not engage regularly in conversational relationships with others.

What is this doing, except saying in longer words what the parents already knew when they brought the child in for evaluation in the first place—that the child was late in talking?

There are various other labels that have some meaning, but which labels may or may not apply to the particular child. "Pervasive developmental disorder" is a label often applied to children whose development is perfectly normal, or even more advanced than that of others their age, but which lags in just one area. It is a sign of the power of pat phrases that something can be regarded as "pervasive" when it is in fact confined to a single isolated problem. Sometimes the child's only problem is that outsiders have declared that he has a problem, even though he gets along fine at home and the family has no trouble dealing with him.

Pervasive developmental disorder (PDD) is often spoken of as part of, or related to, autism. However, one of the leading authorities on autism, Dr. Bernard Rimland of the Autism Research Institute in San Diego, calls the term "uninformative" and "confusing," and says that it "should be abandoned." He says that parents "want to know the truth, insofar as the truth is known" and adds: "If we don't know the right label for their child, let's tell them that up front, rather than hide our ignorance behind the mystique of a pseudo-scientific label, presuming knowledge we don't have, like PDD."[9] As regards autism in general, Dr. Rimland says: "In recent years autism has become fashionable, and the term is vastly over-used."[10]

Such candor is especially refreshing coming from a scholar who has spent many years specializing in the study of autism. What is truly appalling is that so many other people have a know-it-all attitude in an area where no one knows nearly enough.

Another label often applied with abandon is "attention deficit hyperactivity disorder." Whatever this might mean if carefully defined and selectively applied, it is too often applied like ketchup, to almost anything. In some cases, it can mean nothing more than the fact that a bright child is bored by a dull teacher or unchallenging material. Too often the child is put on medication, instead of being presented with an education capable of engaging the attention of someone with an active or gifted mind.

A parent might be well advised to try another class or another school before trying Ritalin. Some parents of late-talking children have reported almost miraculous changes in their child just from finding a better teacher or a better school environment.

Unfortunately, the generally low intellectual level of teachers in the public schools—documented by decades of research[11]—is a major obstacle to finding a challenging environment for a bright child. While some have argued that it does not take much intellect to teach the first grade or kindergarten, what such arguments overlook is that an intellectual *orientation* matters, even when presenting elementary material. Bright children, especially, may respond with fascination to the logic of mathematics, but be bored to death by silly "activities" and "projects" with numbers dreamed up by teachers with no intellectual orientation.

A popular handbook for parents lists among the "warning signals" for young children with speech delay that they use "gestures or noises to indicate wants."[12] What else would they do, if they can't talk? Contrary to what this particular handbook claims, a professor with an endowed chair in the Department of Audiology and Speech Sciences at Purdue University reports research findings that "children who caught up to peers in language development had made active use of gestures to assist communications."[13]

Terms such as "apraxia" or "hyperlexia" have specific meanings and yet may be used far beyond the area in which those meanings apply. Too often the official *Diagnostic and Statistical Manual of Mental Disorders* is cited as if it represented scientific certainty, rather than a committee-written compendium with widely varying mixtures of hard facts and fashionable speculations.[14]

Perhaps even more troubling than the nebulous nature of some labels, or the inaccuracy with which they may be applied to a particular child, is the indelibility of such labels and their following the child for years, or even decades, into and out of the school system. Assurances made to parents about the "confidentiality" of these labels may mean much less than they seem to.

Confidentiality does not mean anonymity. Records containing such labels remain identifiable by name, even when that information is officially classified as "confidential." Assurances that this information will not be given to any "unauthorized" individual or organization are absolutely meaningless, because anyone that this information is given to will be labeled "authorized." Such assurances are mere tautologies which say that the information will be given only to those to whom it is given. Stephen Camarata summarized the reality of the situation in his advice to a parent: "There is no such thing as a confidential file."

Chapter 6

"Early Intervention"

"E arly intervention" covers a wide range of options for trying to get a child to begin talking. There is also another option often recommended by pediatricians who find a child medically unimpaired and obviously bright—be patient and let him develop at his own pace. That was essentially Professor Hamilton's advice to me when my son was not talking. Obviously, everything depends on the particular child and the particular circumstances. Unfortunately, there are zealots for whom "early intervention" is not one option to be weighed against others but a battle cry in a crusade for all. Yet scientists and scholars who have studied children with speech delays have reached more measured conclusions. For example, a prominent British authority observed:

> On the one hand, it might seem desirable to initiate therapy as early as possible to give the child the best opportunity of overcoming the impairment before starting school. On the other hand, the disorder might resolve naturally, and treatment could create more problems

than it solves by producing low expectations in teachers, anxiety in parents, and self-consciousness in the child.[1]

Nothing caused such shrill denunciations of *Late-Talking Children* when it was first published, four years ago—including denunciations from people who admitted that they had not read it—as its suggestion that "early intervention" was not always the best thing and that sometimes it did harm. Nor were critics appeased when I said in my newspaper column: "There is no need to be for or against early intervention on a blanket basis. Everything depends on the particular situation and the particular child." That just set off more angry letters to me and, in at least one case, to a newspaper that carried my syndicated column.

Unless "early intervention" is a panacea, common sense would require us to consider its pros and cons in each given case. No responsible parent is going to do nothing while a child remains silent past his second, third or fourth birthday, even though some speech therapists and others have depicted the alternative to early intervention as doing nothing. Having medical and intelligence tests done and getting the best medical advice possible is not "doing nothing," even if that advice is ultimately to let this particular child develop at his own pace. Of all the late-talking adults I have met or heard of, including many who turned out to be high achievers, none had early intervention.

Where there are real reasons to fear more serious problems than a temporary speech delay, then of course something should be done—and done as soon as possible. Unfortunately, "early intervention" is a catch-all phrase that covers all sorts of very different actions, programs and techniques, run by people at all levels of competence and incompetence. Some of these people and programs have had very bad results for particular children, while others have been a godsend.

As already seen in Chapter 3, the twin girls in Alabama were shunted off into classes for children with very different problems, where their own academic development was completely neglected for years, despite their ability to do higher level work at home. Billy in California was thrown in with autistic children. Joshua in Arizona retrogressed dramatically after just one day in a special class for children with learning disabilities. Andy in New York began speaking suddenly *after* being removed from a special class whose teachers were described by his mother as "the most rude, nastiest and most insensitive" she had ever encountered. Many of the letters I received from other parents after *Late-Talking Children* was published told very similar stories. A mother who described herself as "desperate" on the Internet had a five-year old whose speech development was behind schedule and who comes back from speech therapy sessions saying "Talk, talk, talk, you dumb boy." He also became physically aggressive in what his mother feared was a re-enactment of what he has been through in the therapy sessions. Another parent, whose son's speech therapy sessions are conducted in her home, reports that her little boy runs away into another room when he sees the therapist approaching the house. None of this is at all like my experience with the excellent young lady at Ithaca College who gave speech therapy to my son while his mother and I watched through one-way glass.

A mother in Dallas wrote to me in August 1997 that her son "became so negative six weeks into his first speech therapy setting that I removed him, feeling deeply that it was doing more harm than good." However, she changed to a different speech therapy, conducted in her home in her presence, and insisted that "the sessions last only as long as he willingly participates, and are always fun and positive." Another mother, whose child was thrown in with autistic children, found him to be fearful of their strange and sometimes violent behavior, and to become more withdrawn from other children in general.

Again, "early intervention" covers the good, the bad and the ugly, so one cannot be for or against it on a blanket basis. Nor can one take seriously a guidebook for parents that says, "You have nothing to lose by seeking help."[2] You and your child have a lot to lose, if you are not careful and skeptical with people who have a vested interest in promoting intervention.

It is not just with me that the "early intervention" establishment is vigilant in defense of its turf. After a mother wrote an essay in the March/April 1997 issue of *Family Life* magazine about how her daughter outgrew her speech problems, school psychologists from California and Tennessee wrote letters to the editor, warning that "early identification and treatment are critical" and that "letting things work themselves out in a child like this could have drastic effects developmentally."[3] How this psychologist could possibly know what "a child like this" was, without ever having seen her, is a question with painful implications for the recklessness with which some professionals reach conclusions. Many of the critics who wrote me likewise did not hesitate to diagnose children they had never seen, including not only children mentioned in the book but also various other children and adults, including Microsoft mogul Bill Gates, whom one of these "experts" diagnosed as autistic![4]

Even after having encountered know-it-all dogmatism among speech therapists and others in the stories told by many of the parents in our group, it was still a shock to me to discover, from the additional mail that came in after the book was published, how many "professionals" were willing to shoot from the hip on something as momentous as the future development of a child.

Although school conferences to determine where to place a child in school are referred to as "individual educational program" (IEP) conferences, all too often they are attempts to fill existing programs with children, rather than to deal with the individual child's particular situation. Moreover, the legal safeguards established to allow parents the right to refuse particular labels or particular programs may not be explained to these parents, who may be left to believe that they have no choice but to go along with the "experts."

While some children have actually retrogressed under some forms of early intervention, the deeper and more long-lasting damage may be to the child's conception of himself and of his relationship with his family. Being constantly pressed to talk before he is ready can drive home the message that he is a big disappointment to his parents. One couple who were sunk in despair over the failure of their young daughter to speak sat around one evening, pouring out their sorrow to one another, as if the little girl could not hear or understand what they were saying. Then the little toddler spoke her first words: "I'm sorry." No child needs to be made to feel like that.

One mother—not a member of our group—wrote to me that reading *Late-Talking Children* "made me very thankful to be 62 and to have had children before there were so many 'experts' around." Her daughter did not start talking until she was three and a half years old. However, her parents "did not become alarmed at any time about Ann's not talking, nor did we have her in day care or preschool to enable any 'expert' to become alarmed about the situation." Now in her thirties, Ann is a Certified Public Accountant. Both her parents are engineers.

A letter from another parent outside our groups showed that it is by no means easy to get the educational establishment to accept an arrangement tailored to the particular child, rather than one conforming to the educators' general notions:

> I cannot tell you the stir I caused when I came to the IEP meeting armed with an outside educator's assessment of Bessie which

asserted that she would be successful in regular classes with minimal support. You would have thought that I had personally wounded these teachers. I asked that Bessie "repeat" kindergarten but do so in a regular class. This sent the meeting into such a tailspin that they actually stopped the meeting and said, "well we'll have to convene later." The educators in charge of Bessie's placement did nothing in the intervening months. I meanwhile interviewed the principals of 2 local elementary schools, arranged for Bessie to attend summer school one day in a regular kindergarten session and another in a first grade class and successfully negotiated her placement at that school for the fall in regular kindergarten. She has been successful and supported in her efforts there ever since. When the educators finally reconvened I presented them with a fait accompli and included the regular kindergarten teacher in the session. Since the principal had observed Bessie in his kindergarten and first grade classes, and the kindergarten teacher had already agreed that she would teach Bessie, there was little the establishment could do. Lord help those children whose parents are unable to negotiate within the educational system or who are too intimidated to try.

Miracle cures for late-talking abound, both in non-profit institutions and in private businesses charging hefty fees. Even when parents are assured that "studies prove" the effectiveness of this or that method, those studies may be often done by the very people who run these programs or by consultants or others associated with the programs. Such studies may be published or cited in reputable publications, but the original source is what determines whether it is objective science or disguised advertising.

Although I have received many heart-warming letters of appreciation from parents of late-talking children, there was also a bitter letter from a mother whose son turned out to be autistic and who blamed me for her not having gotten him treated earlier:

You do the public a disservice by your article. I read it the first time and thought my boy was just a late-talker. After all, the doctor said the same.

Unfortunately, he has autism and apraxia . . .

I wish I had never read your first article. You were fortunate things turned out well for you. You were just *another obstacle* to getting [my son] who is 6 years old into an appropriate therapy program.

Rather than risk having anyone else misinterpret what I have said, let me be very clear that no one should simply *assume* that any given child is like the children discussed in this book. Given the uncertain state of current knowledge on this subject, the message should not be complacency but just the opposite: Seek multiple and truly independent diagnoses from the best qualified professionals available. The dangers from being wrong—in either direction—are too great to rely on school-supplied individuals or teams, or on anybody with professional ties to public or private programs that need a continuing supply of clients.

Autism is a particular danger. The fact that its symptoms include characteristics also found to some degree in high-IQ children in general, and especially among children with the Einstein syndrome in particular, makes it urgently important for parents to get the best and most unbiased professional evaluations possible. Unfortunately, the very definition of autism has increasingly become surrounded with a penumbra of uncertainty and inconsistency. The classic autistic individual depicted in the movie *Rain Man* may be at the core of the concept but the term has been expanded both in theory and in practice. The existence of government-provided money and services has been one reason for applying the label more loosely to children who bear little or no resemblance to the *Rain Man* character.

It may well be that autism is related to other unusual phenomena, in which case the term "autistic spectrum" may be applicable—or autism might be considered part of some other spectrum, with other regions of that spectrum presenting nothing like the severe social problems associated with autism. In short, there is no such scientific certainty as to preclude honest differences of opinion and varying definitions among specialists. However, this situation can be a minefield for parents. Nevertheless, minefields sometimes have to be crossed. But choosing a reliable guide is crucial, preferably one who does not talk in broad labels, but in terms of a highly specific diagnosis and prognosis for a particular child.

Since children who talk late do so for such a wide variety of reasons—including deafness, mental retardation, and autism—generalizations about them may not be very useful for the parents of any given child. Those who evaluate late-talking children may be aware that children who talk late tend to average lower IQs and poorer academic performances than "normal" children and to have other continuing problems when tested or evaluated years later. However, studies which break down this broad, heterogenous category into (1) those who neither speak nor understand when spoken to, and (2) those who understand quite well but just do not talk, show that the latter turn out well far more often than the former.

A study of late-talking children in England found that those three-year-olds whose only problem was that they were not yet talking were doing well by age five and a half in more than three quarters of the cases. However, those who neither spoke nor understood what was said to them were doing well by the same age only 14 percent of the time.[5] A study in New Zealand likewise found that those who simply were not talking at age three "were not a high-risk group for later problems," while those who could neither speak nor understand speech were.[6]

These general patterns may be helpful for putting things in perspective, though they can never be conclusive for any given child. Knowing such patterns may enable parents to resist those who try to stampede them into special programs by claiming that delayed speech automatically means big trouble down the road. However, the fact that most children who do understand speech without being able to speak themselves usually turn out all right does not mean that all do. Nor, for that matter, does the fact that most children who neither speak nor understand speech usually do have more serious and long-lasting problems mean that all such children will turn out badly. Clara Schumann said that she neither spoke nor understood speech until she was four years old.

Even when a late-talking child's speech development proceeds to evolve by itself until normal speech is finally achieved, the time that this takes and the side-effects this can produce are serious things to consider. The parents in the group that I studied usually became concerned over their children's failure to begin talking when these children were two years old. Since the average age at which the children in this group were beginning to really talk—as distinguished from saying isolated words—was age four, this meant that these parents went through an average of two years of very anxious waiting and foreboding.

This much stress cannot be good for anybody and it might even affect the relationship between parent and child, with lasting consequences. It can also affect the relationship between husband and wife. In two of the families in my group, sharp parental differences in their assessments of the child's prospects were cited as factors in their divorces. A father from outside the group phoned me to credit *Late-Talking Children* with saving his marriage because he and his wife had been at such loggerheads over their late-talking daughter—or rather, over whether to accept dire diagnoses about her. By the time he phoned, the little girl was talking and was doing fine in school.

There can also be lasting effects on the child's social development, if he acquires the habit of withdrawal from social contacts during the period when he is unable to communicate. Attempts to improvise words can also leave verbal habits that have to be un-learned later. As a 1925 study of a late-talking little girl found:

> Although R could and did use many proper terms, through force of habit she continued the incorrect ones. Her speech development was top-heavy—it was characterized by rapid addition of words but by a poor technique of sentence structure; her incorrect habits acquired through her period of delayed speed development hampered her in her period of rapid development. It was not until she was past four and a half that her sentence structures were correct and complete. Thus it took her a year and a half after she became willing to talk for her to master the main correct speaking forms—inflections, the verb "to be," etc.[7]

Such verbal problems created by letting a child's speech development take its own course may be overshadowed by other problems and dangers. After all, once a child is speaking normally, no one he encounters in later life will care when it happened.

Another aspect of the situation that needs to be considered is that of discipline. Many parents of children who are not talking, and whose general level of comprehension is uncertain, are understandably reluctant to impose the same discipline on a child who may be incapable of understanding as they would impose on their other children. If speeding up the child's speech development helps resolve questions about his comprehension, then that child may be prevented from becoming an uncontrollable brat or someone whose lack of self-discipline can create lasting problems for himself.

Whether the possibility of lasting problems associated with delayed speech outweigh the lasting harm that can be done by some forms of "early intervention" can only be assessed by parents who very carefully consider all aspects of their own child's situation. And even the most carefully considered decision can turn out to be wrong and harmful. That is the inescapable burden of being a parent, whether your child is late in talking or not. All that you can know is that you did your best.

SUMMARY AND IMPLICATIONS

It is perhaps inevitable that there will be much uncertainty in the evaluations of a rare group of children who are both very bright and very late in beginning to speak, especially since the very existence of a set of such children with their own distinctive intellectual and social patterns has only recently been discovered. However, it is certainty, rather than uncertainty, which has caused much needless distress to parents and much counterproductive treatment of children. Hasty and dogmatic conclusions have been all too widespread among both laymen and professionals.

Often anything unusual about late-talking children has been seized upon as an explanation for their not talking. For example, ear infections have been blamed for delayed speech development, on the assumption that resulting hearing problems must have caused the speaking problems. This may in fact happen sometimes but that is very different from simply jumping to the conclusions that this is the cause with any particular child. Sometimes two languages are spoken in the home and this is then assumed to be the reason for the child's delay in speaking. However, cases have been reported to me where children in such situations, after they begin to talk, speak in both languages and with no apparent confusion between them. Even before beginning to speak, they have responded to directions in both languages. A bilingual home is no more certain to have caused speech delays than ear infections are.

Even when there is no tangible evidence of anything whatever to blame for a child's delayed speech development, causes have simply been assumed—not enough reading to the child, not enough discipline, too much anticipation of the child's needs . . . and so on and on. Mothers are especially likely to be targeted for blame. Lack of knowledge is only part of the problem. As Will Rogers said, "It's not ignorance that is so bad. It is all the things we know that ain't so."

The painful reality must be recognized that some professionals and semi-professionals like playing the role of little tin gods, whose word is not to be questioned, least of all by parents whose first-hand observations and views are sweepingly dismissed as the pathology of people "in denial." A neurologist whose hasty diagnosis was questioned replied that he had diagnosed thousands of children—but the relevant question was how often had his diagnoses proved to be right, and how often wrong, as shown by the future development of these children. The very thought of keeping such records would not occur to many evaluators. Fortunately, Professor Camarata's ongoing study at Vanderbilt will follow the children in his group into adulthood, providing the first solid evidence on how often the "experts" are right and how often they turn out to be wrong. In the meantime, skepticism and second opinions are very much in order.

To say that the evaluation of bright children who talk late is not a science would be to understate the problem considerably. There are in fact two very different problems: (1) the inadequacies of the current state of knowledge on this newly researched phenomenon and (2) the haste and dogmatism with which labels are too often applied. Research in progress at Vanderbilt University can do much to alleviate the first problem, but only a greater awareness of the emerging facts on the part of parents and professionals alike has any chance of making headway against the second.

Chapter 7

Coping with Uncertainties

The uncertainties surrounding late-talking children are both short run and long run. Parents who have all they can do to cope with current anxieties and stresses may have little time and energy left to devote to contemplating the very different considerations that will have to be faced after their child is speaking normally and has normal—or above normal—intellectual development. For those children with the Einstein syndrome, their special abilities can present a problem, as well as an opportunity. Parents may need to become especially aware of this because too many schools have little or no interest in developing the special abilities of such children. Indeed, those abilities can cause both educational and social problems. Einstein himself was regarded as a problem student and his departure was hastened.

Before proceeding to these long-run problems, we need to consider one of the earliest problems faced by parents of late-talking children—when to introduce them to preschools, kindergartens or other institutional settings.

INSTITUTIONS AND SOCIAL
DEVELOPMENT

Many young children are put into various institutions such as nursery schools and kindergartens for their own social development. Some are put into such places because both parents work. In either case, the decision is worth a careful assessment of how much is gained and how much is lost—especially when the child is late in talking.

Most of the problems of late-talking children occur outside the home and especially in institutional settings. Such children encounter many problems in preschool programs, not only because of their inability to communicate, but also because their tendency toward highly individualistic behavior clashes with the routines and rigidities of institutions.

Late-talking children may have difficulties and frictions not only with the adults who are seeking to create a structured routine but also with other children, whether because of shyness on the part of the late-talkers or because they are shunned by other children who do not understand them. Adults who deal with late-talking children may also create special problems for them or their parents because of these adults' tendencies to label the children or because they simply do not know how to handle them.

On the other hand, the child may need to be with other children, in order to foster his own social development. This may be especially important when the late-talker is the only child in the family and there are few or no children of his age in the neighborhood. However, everything depends not only on the particular child's circumstances but also on his own stage of development. Putting a child into a social setting that he is not yet ready to handle may only foster a habit of withdrawal from new people that long outlasts the initial situation and persists long after the child is speaking fluently and would otherwise be able to function well in social settings.

Just as throwing him into the ocean will not make him swim, so putting him into social surroundings before he is ready will not automatically create the skills needed to cope with those surroundings. While many will urge that socialization outside the home is essential, that in itself says nothing about the age at which it should occur or what the prerequisites are to make it helpful, rather than harmful. A child who is not talking, or whose speech development is far behind that of other children, can easily become not only unsettled within himself but also can become disdained or even targeted by his peers. Indeed such a child may become targeted by adults primed to "recognize" various "disorders" that they have been told about by "experts."

THE LONGER RUN

Our focus so far has been on the early years, when children with the Einstein syndrome are either not talking or are lagging behind other children their age in speech development and in the social development that goes along with verbal interactions with other children and adults. Although this is a stage that rightly arouses great parental concerns, it is nevertheless a stage which most bright children who talk late eventually outgrow. What they do not usually outgrow are their outstanding analytical abilities. This can be a plus in their education and their future lives, but it can also be a school problem that lasts much longer than the early years of anxiety about their delayed speech development.

The uneven development of many of the children with the Einstein syndrome can cause them to be misunderstood by teachers and others, as Einstein himself was, and as children in my group and in Professor Camarata's have been. Sometimes this unevenness is between different intellectual areas—mathematics versus poetry, for example—but often it is a broader unevenness between intellectual development and social development. Very bright children in general—whether they talk late or not—face their own peculiar problems in schools geared toward students with much less intellectual ability than they have. "Many gifted students" who are intellectually mismatched with the other students around them are reported to be "isolated and lonely," and to be regarded by teachers and classmates as "smart alecks," "class clowns," or "misfits."[1] Professor Julian Stanley of Johns Hopkins University, who created a program for mathematically precocious children, has argued that ordinarily there is "no *suitable* way to while away the class hours" for such children, who suffer boredom and frustration, and tend to develop "habits of gross inattention."[2]

Quite aside from social problems caused by late speech development, children with above average levels of intelligence in general tend to be "loners" more often than children whose intelligence falls within the average or normal range. This is not new. An 1894 study of the childhoods of eminent men found solitary play to have been more common among them than among other children. Later studies found solitary activities to be especially prevalent among children with very high IQs, along with a tendency to become "isolated" in general and to have "struggles" against "dull or otherwise unworthy adults in authority" over them—which can lead to "contempt for authority wherever it is found," including the authority of parents.[3]

Where a child like those in the groups studied here has intelligence that is far beyond that of his peers and far ahead of what his school work is geared to, that can be a problem which endures for years beyond the point where his speech becomes normal. Some of the negative personality traits seen in gifted children in general may not be separate traits, as such, but emotional reactions to an unusual situation which most other people do not face. Whether such a child would develop the same personality traits in a school or class geared to children of similar ability levels and in a social setting where he would encounter many other children of his own ability level is another question.

Studies have shown youngsters with very high IQs in general to be less popular with their peers than either average youngsters or youngsters with moderately high IQs. Not surprisingly, loneliness and emotional problems tend to be more common among children with very high levels of intellectual ability. Moreover, the friendships that are formed by children with very high IQs tend to be with other youngsters with similar IQs—when such are available—or with children older than themselves or with adults.[4] In short, the social problems of gifted children seem to be a result of the intellectual *disparities* between themselves and their age-peers, rather than being intrinsic anti-social patterns among the gifted.

Envy and resentment by less able students—or even by teachers, as Edward Teller's experience as a child illustrates—are other sources of social and emotional maladjustments experienced by children with unusually high intelligence. Moreover, "schools tend to reward quiet, neat students who do as they are told."[5] These are not the usual characteristics of high-IQ youngsters in general or those with the Einstein syndrome in particular. A study of children with IQs of 180 and up contained bitter episodes of their clashes with teachers who were mediocrities.[6]

It may be very difficult—perhaps impossible—to separate out just how much of a child's unusual behavior is due to the unusual circumstances he finds himself in and how much represents problems innate to that individual. These unusual circumstances can include late talking as well as high IQs, and of course this applies doubly when a child is both very bright and has delayed speech development.

The exceptionally intelligent child faces not only special social problems in school but also special academic problems. Again, none of this is new. A 1942 study found that children with very high IQs "are likely to regard school with indifference, or with positive distaste, for they find nothing interesting to do there." Even their special intellectual abilities were likely to go to waste as such students receive "daily practice in habits of idleness and daydreaming," while the ease with which they glide through the school work tends to build "expectations of an effortless existence,"[7] so that they do not develop the necessary study habits and self-discipline required to bring their mental potential to fruition.

Children with IQs of 140 were found to be able to "master all the mental work provided in the elementary school, as established, in half the time allowed"[8]—and this was in 1942, decades before the "dumbing down" of the schools in the 1960s and afterwards. More recent studies have shown intellectually precocious children to be able to master a year of high school work in just three months in the Johns Hopkins summer programs for such children.[9]

While loneliness and emotional problems have been common in childhood and adolescence among very intellectually precocious individuals, such problems have not been nearly as common in adulthood. What is different about adulthood is that they are now "able to find others like themselves" as Professor Winner pointed out in her study of gifted children.[10] Unlike the schools, where their associates are selected for them by others, in adulthood they are freer to go into fields, occupations, and activities where they encounter more people with whom they no longer have such large intellectual disparities.

A similar reduction of intellectual differences is possible in the schools, but it seldom happens, even though this could have educational as well as social benefits. Among the possible ways of reducing intellectual disparities between very bright children and their classmates are letting such children skip grades individually or grouping such individuals into classes of children with similarly high abilities and providing an education geared to their intellectual level. An intermediate possibility might be to let the gifted child take particular courses—mathematics, for example—with older children, while remaining with age-peers for other subjects in which differences in ability are not so pronounced.

Unfortunately, there is great resistance within the education establishment to all these ways of developing the special talents of outstanding students and sparing them the social maladjustments that often accompany their high intellectual level. Even school activities labeled "gifted and talented" programs often have no accelerated or deeper intellectual content. Too often, they have merely extra busy work or social activities designed to produce attitudes considered desirable by the education establishment.

Despite sweeping assertions by many educators that individual acceleration or ability grouping creates social maladjustments, empirical studies have shown no such thing.[11] A scholar who reviewed numerous studies reported:

> More than two hundred articles that I have examined report experiences of students who have, in one way or another, been advanced in school because they appeared to be academically ready for a challenge beyond their years. Some reported on students who were granted early admission in kindergarten or first grade, others on students who skipped one or more grades, and still others on students who earned college credit while in high school or who entered college early. Not one of these studies lends credence to the notion that such practices lead to major difficulties for the students involved. It is, indeed, much easier from the available evidence to make the case that students who are allowed to move ahead according to their competencies are benefited in their social and emotional development than it is to make the case that they are harmed.[12]

The almost pathetic gratitude expressed by youngsters who attended a special summer program for bright children at Purdue University, and the painful contrasts they drew between this program and what they have to put up with—both academically and psychologically—in their regular schools suggest that a setting geared to their needs could be enormously beneficial.[13]

When intellectually more able students are forced to learn at a slower pace and at a shallower level geared to average students, that is more than a waste of the child's potential. It can be a source of lasting intellectual problems, as well as the social problems already noted. Intellectually, the easiness of the work for a child with very high abilities provides no reason for that child to develop good study habits or to learn to persevere and apply himself in the face of difficulties. As the scholar quoted above put it:

> The child for whom everything comes easily may learn to expect that everything *should* come easily. He or she may be made anxious and discouraged when faced with a degree of challenge or even a minor failure that a less capable student would take in stride. Encounters with adversity may have devastating effects, including avoidance of difficulty, feelings of self-abasement, and even withdrawal from college or graduate study.[14]

A curriculum that is far too easy for such a child can lead to habits of tuning out and turning off. The boredom and restlessness of such children when presented with material far below their intellectual level, or at a pace far slower than their learning rate, is all too easily labeled "attention deficit hyperactivity disorder" or some other jargon that blames the child for the school's inadequacies or rigidities.

It is hard to escape the conclusion that many educators resist providing special education for gifted youngsters out of a lockstep conception of human development, an ideological bias against "elitism," or a lack of empathy for children so different intellectually from the kinds of people who predominate in the field of education. Envy and resentment should also not be ruled out as factors in the education establishment's often bitter resistance to accommodating very bright children, as they accommodate various other kinds of children who differ from the norm.[15]

Parents might well consider finding schools, classes, or teachers geared to the kind of child they have—and especially avoid those who would try to drug their child (with Ritalin, for example) into becoming the kind of child that the existing institutional setting is designed to accommodate. That comes dangerously close to the myth of the Procrustean bed, in which the body was mutilated to fit the furniture. Those who seek to drug children risk mutilating the mind and spirit to fit a rigid educational system.

Sometimes the problems are not confined to institutions and professionals. Sometimes the parents themselves have rigidly unrealistic expectations. One mother who went on the Internet to comment on *Late-Talking Children* said:

> My own son was a late talker. He did not produce intelligible, grammatical speech until he was almost four. He is a very right-hemisphere child who would easily fit Sowell's group. However, and importantly, he cannot read as well as he can use a computer, play chess, build things, or do his older sister's math homework. I do not consider this trivial. I WOULD WANT HIM TO BE ABLE TO ENJOY LITERATURE, POETRY AND DRAMA AS WELL AS COMPUTE. LATE-TALKERS ARE NOT OK JUST BECAUSE THEY NOW TALK INTELLIGIBLY.

One can only feel sorry for a child whose mother has such a set of demands, as if she could order a son from the factory to her own specifications and ready to become a Renaissance man. She did not even claim that her son cannot read well, but that he cannot read *as well as* he can do math, use a computer, or play chess. Few people excel at everything across the board, whether or not they talk late. Fortunately, most parents are happy to have children with varying interests and talents, because that is the way most children—and most adults—are. Many of the parents who are currently deeply worried about their child's delayed speech would be grateful beyond words to have their child turn out as well as this little boy whose mother is complaining.

PARTING THOUGHTS

Many of the practical day-to-day problems and stresses that go along with delayed speech development in young children are far more acute in institutions than in the home. Yet, even where there is a stay-at-home mom and other children in the home or neighborhood for her child to play with, the pervasive pattern of putting children into some institution early on may cause this decision to be made without much serious weighing of the many factors that deserve to be considered.

No one knows how the children in either of the groups studied here will turn out. Some may turn out to be normal, average adults. Others may have lifelong problems, even after learning to speak. Still others—perhaps the majority—will go on to have distinguished achievements, like many such children who have gone before them. It will be well into the third millennium before the results are all in on the individuals being studied. Even then, no given parent with a given child can know what that particular child's future holds. On the other hand, neither do the parents of so-called "normal" children. All must live on love and hope—and these have had a pretty good track record for a very long time.

Epilogue:
Related Thoughts

Some of the afterthoughts and implications of this study that may be worth considering are:

1. How were these special children discovered and when did they begin to be studied?
2. How have professionals such as speech therapists responded to the publication of this study?
3. What are some of the wider implications of these findings beyond bright children who talk late?

ORIGINS OF THE STUDY

The systematic study of bright children who talk late began only within the decade of the 1990s, beginning with my book *Late-Talking Children*, and continuing on an expanded scale with the research of Professor Stephen Camarata of Vanderbilt University. There was a book about one such girl back in 1974—*The Slow Speech Development of a Bright Child* by Thelma Weeks—and an article about another such girl, nearly half a century earlier, in 1925.[1]

But there was no study of a whole group of such children until *Late-Talking Children* was published in 1997.

Why was this special subset of late-talking children not discovered before? Perhaps one clue is the wholly accidental way in which I stumbled across them and only belatedly realized that they shared other characteristics besides delayed speech development.

My research on late-talking children came about not only accidentally, but even reluctantly. In May 1993, when my son graduated from college, I wrote about him in my syndicated newspaper column, mentioning that he was nearly four years old before he began to speak and noting also his unusual analytical abilities and remarkable memory.

Letters began to come in from around the country from parents and grandparents of children with very similar characteristics.

They wanted me to tell them why children who seemed so bright were years late in talking and what they could do about it. But I could tell them nothing about either of these things. However, as someone who knew from personal experience what anxieties they were going through, I wrote back that I would search the literature for some books or articles on such children that they might read. The first of many surprises awaiting me was that *there were no such books or articles*. There were many writings on late-talking children in general, but my research assistant and I found nothing specifically about bright children who talk late.

At first, I thought that we were just looking in the wrong places. But months of searching by hand and by computer still produced nothing. So did a later search directed by noted language authority Professor Steven Pinker of M.I.T., who was kind enough to help me in this and other ways.

By September 1993, I had to admit that I had drawn a complete blank. However, rather than leave the anxious parents completely high and dry, I offered them an opportunity to exchange addresses with one another through me, so that they could share their experiences with one another and at least end the sense of utter isolation that so many parents felt—and which I had felt when my son was late in talking. Thus an informal network of a couple of dozen families was formed that later grew to 55 families scattered across 24 states from coast to coast. Parents whose children were still delayed in learning to speak seemed particularly relieved to hear from those parents whose children were now grown and doing fine.

In the course of reading the many letters that circulated within our group and sometimes talking with parents on the phone, I began to sense that this was not a typical cross-section of people, any more than their children were typical. Still, this was just a general impression of mine. Months passed before it finally occurred to me to survey the group, in order to determine whether there might be a pattern here.

If any particular thing turned my thoughts in this direction, it was a mother who mentioned in passing that her husband was a pilot in the Marine Corps. I had recently learned of other pilots in the families of other late-talking children, so it struck me that there seemed to be a lot of pilots for a group this size. When the results of the survey came in, the big story turned out not to be pilots, but engineers. This made a special impact on me because my brother is an engineer.

Now that I had data showing unusual patterns among both the children and their families, it seemed to me that this was something that should be pursued further by someone with expertise in this general area, since my only professional training was in economics. However, months of attempts to get medical, scientific, or other authorities interested in taking over this research were wholly unsuccessful.

The one benefit that came out of all my futile efforts came from the unlikely process of simply writing a letter to the author of the best-selling book *The Language Instinct*. This was Professor Steven Pinker of M.I.T., who turned out to be enormously helpful to me by discussing some of the possible implications of what I had found and by having one of his graduate students send me an annotated bibliography of relevant scientific writings.

These writings and discussions with Professor Pinker buttressed my own preliminary conclusions, based on previous readings about brain research. But Steven Pinker's input gave me the confidence to proceed, without fearing that my beliefs were just the natural bias of an economist toward thinking "there is no free lunch" in the brain. Moreover, the fact that other anomalies among highly intelligent people were attributed by neuroscientists to a disproportionate distribution of brain resources to intellectual uses meant that it required no great originality on my part to see speech delays among bright children as perhaps part of the same pattern.

Because children can talk late for a wide variety of reasons, it is very doubtful whether most children with delayed speech development fit the Einstein syndrome. Those who do may be lost in a sea of those who don't. It is hard to imagine how this special subset of children could have been discovered, except accidentally. Only the responses of many parents to my newspaper column about my son began to sort out these kinds of children from children whose speech was delayed for other reasons.

Eventually, I realized that, if a study of these children was going to be done, I was the one who would have to do it. In 1996, I sent out a larger and more comprehensive survey questionnaire, based on additional reading I had done, to the families in the group. The book was written that year, beginning with a candid statement on the first page that I was "someone who has no pretensions to scientific or medical expertise."

My later published discussions of similar children in newspaper and magazine articles then prompted more parents of such children to bring them to my attention or to the attention of Professor Camarata at Vanderbilt. A "Dateline.NBC" feature on such special late-talking children, broadcast on March 17, 1999, brought another flood of messages from parents of such children to Stephen Camarata and to me. In short, these were pre-selected children who reached us—selected by their own parents, not only on the basis of delayed speech, but also in many cases because they showed the other characteristics now summarized as the Einstein syndrome.

It is doubtful whether any of this could have happened, except very recently in history, and it is doubtful whether it could happen today in many other countries around the world. Consider, for example, the unusual occupational patterns in the families of these children. Most people with the innate ability to become engineers, mathematicians or scientists have only recently had sufficient access to higher education to make this a reality, even in the United States. Therefore the striking occupational patterns found among the relatives of children with the Einstein syndrome would not have been visible, except within the past two generations, even among Americans, much less in countries where access to higher education remains restricted to a small elite.

Now that these children have been discovered, however accidentally, there is a need not only for further research but also for further dissemination of existing knowledge about these children to parents, as well as to various professionals working with children. Turf-conscious resistance to new information in this area, by lower-level practitioners especially, makes it particularly important that parents become aware of what has been discovered thus far and what new results emerge from the ongoing work of Professor Camarata, who will be following these children on into adulthood.

REACTIONS OF PROFESSIONALS

What were the reactions of professionals to the findings published in *Late-Talking Children*?

The variations in reactions were enormous. Very generous praise came from Professor Sally Shaywitz of the Yale Medical School, Professor Julian Stanley of Johns Hopkins University, and Professor Steven Pinker of M.I.T. Very hostile responses came from a number of speech therapists and social workers, some of whom admitted that they had not read the book. An Internet web site for specialists in speech development was abuzz with conflicting reactions. Someone teaching at Elms College in Massachusetts posted the following e-mail on the web site in July, 1997:

> Just wanted to alert people that Dateline NBC is thinking about doing a story about Thomas Sowell's "Late-Talking Children" book. Sowell is an economist and doesn't seem to have consulted (or understood) experts. He seems to believe that people who are autistic/PDD can't possibly be intelligent in any way and that therefore people like his son who was a very late talker with poor social skills but very good analytical skills could not possibly merit such a label.

She urged others to contact Dateline NBC, giving phone numbers and fax numbers there, to oppose my "misunderstandings." Fortunately, this e-mail was seen by Professor Steven Pinker, head of a center for cognitive neurosciences at M.I.T. He said the accusations against me "are not fair" and explained why:

> Sowell confesses that he is not an expert in the first sentence of his book. He *has* consulted experts, and cites the primary literature on language delay, autism, gender differences, giftedness, and the development of mathematical and spatial abilities. He does *not* believe that socially unskilled, analytically precocious late talkers are never autistic—on page 2, he writes, "There are some children to whom such labels [retarded, autistic, PDD] legitimately apply, so I do not

want to give these parents (or other parents) false hopes." But he is obviously right that there is no way in the world that his son, and the children like him, are autistic, unless the term is stretched to include anyone who has high analytical and low social skills (in which case a third of my undergraduates, and many of our scientific colleagues, would be labeled autistic).

While distortions and falsifications of what I had said continued from a number of professional sources, perhaps the most discouraging reactions were no reactions at all. At my own expense, I bought more than two hundred copies of *Late-Talking Children* and sent them out to specialists in all 50 states and a few foreign countries. There were no more than half a dozen acknowledgments of receipt of the book. This fitted in with a picture that was emerging from other sources that many professionals—and especially semi-professionals like speech therapists and social workers in schools—had little or no interest in looking at new information and were much more concerned with preserving their turf and their influence with parents.

Late-Talking Children had mentioned many incidents of false diagnoses and counterproductive dogmatism by many of the people who came in contact with bright children who talked late. This clearly did not sit well with those who felt threatened professionally by such revelations. Their hostile responses often did not let facts get in their way.

The climax of these hostile responses came in the December 21, 1999 issue of a newspaper published by the American Speech-Language Hearing Association (ASHA), which announced an organized letter-writing campaign against the ideas expressed in my book and in my syndicated newspaper column. The president of ASHA wrote to newspaper editors around the country, claiming that I was "basing his conclusions only on the experience of his son."[2] This was only one of many demonstrably false statements made by speech therapists in response to my book and my column.

One hostile reviewer, for example, claimed that the "close relatives" of the children in my study included cousins and that the number of musicians and people in analytical occupations was not unusually large among so many relatives. This claim might have made some sense if I had in fact included cousins, which would have produced a much larger number of relatives, but in fact no cousins were counted in my study.

Another critic, who appeared on the March 17, 1999 broadcast on "Dateline.NBC," claimed that my findings about the unusual occupations of the children's relatives were based on a questionnaire which "did not ask how many of these families had people who were writers, artists or people in the social sciences." This was at best misleading. My questionnaire simply left a blank for parents to fill in with their own occupations. There turned out to be one artist and one writer among them. Only for other relatives did I list specific occupations and boxes to check. Here I listed the kinds of occupations that parents had already mentioned in conversations or in letters.

The point of the discussion of family occupations was not to claim that there were no artists, writers, etc., in these families, but to point out the extraordinary over-representation of people in highly analytical occupations. Since this questionnaire was reproduced in the appendix to *Late-Talking Children*, there was no excuse for broadcasting the critic's misleading statements over nationwide television. This particular critic had already voiced her misgivings about the book and about the impending "Dateline.NBC" program on the Internet nearly two years earlier, admitting at that time that she had not yet read the book.[3]

Another disturbing reaction came from owners and promoters of private programs to get children to talk. Their letters were friendly and even sought my endorsement of their programs. As a layman, I had no business endorsing any "cure" for late talking and refused to do so. Those who ran such programs undoubtedly knew that a layman had no business giving endorsements, but they obviously thought that an endorsement from someone who had written a book on the subject could be financially beneficial to them, whether or not it had any validity.

One promoter of such a program referred me to a favorable reference to its results in a well-known book that I had read. However, when I went back to that book and looked up the citation of the study on which its author had relied, that study turned out to have been done by the very man who ran the program and who had written to me. Unfortunately, research done by people with a direct vested interest in a particular method or program are not uncommon, so lofty assertions that "studies prove" this or that can mean much less than meets the eye.

WIDER IMPLICATIONS

The individual and family patterns uncovered in the two studies discussed in this book are basic facts that need to be considered by those who deal with bright children who talk late, regardless of whether further scientific research supports or undermines my particular theory of why those facts are what they are. Now that two substantial samples of such children have been identified, the continuing research of Professor Camarata and others may enlighten us further on this subject in the years ahead. It is of course infinitely more important that the truth emerge from these efforts than that one man's theory be proved or disproved.

What is known already raises some intriguing social questions that reach beyond the parents and children involved. In addition, should research confirm that it is the allocation of brain resources which explains why some very bright children are very delayed in beginning to speak, still more intriguing social questions arise. These include issues revolving around heredity, differences among species, and the role of parents in general.

Heredity and Its Implications

Whatever the cause or causes of the set of characteristics identified here as the Einstein syndrome, it is hard to escape the conclusion that heredity is a major factor. The highly atypical family patterns, showing abilities closely paralleling the abilities precociously developed by bright children who talk late, is just one piece of evidence. A wholly different approach, based on a study of thousands of two-year-olds in Britain, has determined that the environmental explanation of the speech development of most young children in general does not apply to the bottom 5 percent—that is, those who are furthest behind in developing the ability to speak. For this 5 percent—which would include children like many of those in the studies examined here—heredity is the main factor.[4]

In short, studies conducted independently of each other, on entirely different bases, and on opposite sides of the Atlantic, lead toward the same conclusion. Heredity seems clearly to be a predominant factor, whatever the particular mechanisms through which its influence is felt—that is, whether through the organization of the brain or otherwise.

For reasons that go back into history and are aggravated by contemporary controversies, "heredity" is for some people a red flag word that conjures up racial explanations of mental differences. However, the children discussed here include children of black, white, Asian and American Indian ancestry—and these children have both individual and family characteristics very similar to one another, however different they all are from most other children in these various racial and ethnic groups. Heredity is not a code word for race. It is a factor which shifts attention away from such child-rearing practices as anticipating the non-talking child's desires or using two languages in the same home, neither of which has been shown to have any demonstrable effect on the pace at which speech develops.

The particular patterns of abilities found in the two studies reported here may also have some light to shed on an anomaly among black Americans—their over-representation among musicians and under-representation among mathematicians. Various researchers suggest that music and mathematics are highly related skills, as far as the functions of the brain are concerned, and the prevalence of people who play musical instruments among the mathematically or analytically gifted people studied here is certainly consistent with that. Why then, are music and mathematics so differently represented among black Americans?

One of the important social differences between music and mathematics is that mathematics depends on education, while music—especially piano-playing—can be self-taught or picked up from watching others. As late as 1940, most black adults in the United States had not completed elementary school, while there was already a tradition of black musicians going back into the nineteenth century. Even when advanced mathematics belatedly became another possible outlet for talents previously concentrated in music, both the traditions and the social surroundings pointed black young people far more toward music.

The distribution of blacks within music lends support to this explanation. It is precisely in those areas of music requiring little or no formal training—pianos rather than violins, jazz rather than classical music, popular improvisational singing rather than formalized operatic singing—that blacks have not merely held their own but excelled. Whole genres of American music have been crucially influenced or shaped by black musicians, while blacks remain very under-represented in the apparently related field of mathematics and in other fields dependent on mathematics, such as science and engineering.

Blacks may have no more innate ability in music than other groups who have not made nearly as much impact there—or any less in mathematics—but the expression of that ability in narrow channels can lead to spectacular results in those particular channels in which such abilities are concentrated. Nor is this peculiar to blacks. For historical reasons, the Irish have tended to channel much of their talent and ambitions into politics, rather than into scientific or entrepreneurial ventures. In politics, the Irish have like-wise not merely held their own but have had spectacular success. In the heyday of the American big city political machines, the Irish dominated those machines, as they also dominated the leadership of American labor unions. Similar dominance of numerous other fields or occupations by particular racial or ethnic groups have been common in other countries around the world.

Putting aside racial aspects of heredity, what are the implications if it should turn out that our abilities as individuals are heavily influenced by the structures of our brains? It would mean that most of us could never have been like Einstein, no matter how hard we tried, because we simply do not have the brain resources he had. By the same token, many of those who have failed to achieve the intellectual levels that we have achieved may never have had a chance to do so either. If an understanding of this does nothing more than reduce arrogance—and the blindness and cal-lousness that often goes with it—that could be an important social contribution.

Once we recognize that many abilities are inborn, we can aban-don the make-believe equality that American schools are so determined to create at all costs, whether in the way students are grouped, taught, or graded. There is no more reason why the mathematically gifted youngster should be held back and bored by the pace or the material designed for others, who are slower in grasping analytical concepts, than there is for holding back someone whose talents lie in art or writing. One may not be superior to another overall, but each may be superior in different things—and all may be consigned to mediocrity and frustration by lockstep education, based on make-believe equality. It is painfully sobering to think of the very bright children—in this study and elsewhere—who have had serious problems in school, not because they were not very intelligent, but precisely because they were.

The possibility that some children talk late because of precociously developing analytical faculties in their brains does not of course imply the converse—that people with precocious or outstanding analytical abilities must talk late. Most of the high-IQ children in the landmark Terman study at Stanford University tended to begin to speak earlier than normal. Similarly, the preoccupation with music that has been so common among the children studied here need not accompany high-level intellectual ability in general. Nobel Prizewinning economist Milton Friedman, for example, has stated in his memoirs that he was never able to derive any pleasure from music.

It so happens that, the morning after hearing Professor Friedman say the same thing at a dinner, I read about a professor of music who had lost his ability to respond emotionally to music after a brain operation, even though he still retained all his technical knowledge. Could it be that what this professor's brain lost was something that Milton Friedman's brain never had or never developed sufficiently to permit enjoyment of music? Perhaps studies of other such people would shed some light on this. Could a lesser development of this faculty be the price paid by some people for their brain's extraordinary development in other areas, just as other people pay the price in delayed speech development or in immune systems vulnerable to allergies.[5]

Species Differences

The varying allocation of resources within the brain also has implications for comparisons between species. Most animals have far more highly developed senses of smell than human beings do. Being able to make very fine distinctions among scents requires not only a more sensitive nose but also considerable resources in the brain devoted to minutely distinguishing these scents, so as to be able to tell the scent of one species from another and the scent of one individual from another. Those animals whose brains have sufficient resources to do this cannot think as well as human beings, but human beings cannot detect and distinguish scents nearly as well as these animals.

For a deer, it is more crucial to its survival to be able to detect the scent of a lion some distance away than to know that $E = MC^2$. For human beings, a highly developed sense of smell would have no such survival value, since people lack the speed to outrun lions or the strength to fight them. Human survival depends on being able to out-think the lion in various ways, by finding or creating shelters less accessible to lions, lighting fires to repel lions at night, and eventually developing weapons that allow people to hunt lions, instead of vice versa.

Parents

Perhaps the most striking—and inspiring—impression gained from seven years of following bright children who talk late has been the high levels of dedication of the parents of these children.

Some families have strained their financial resources to the breaking point by taking these children to multiple specialists in various parts of the country, in hopes of finding out what is wrong and what can be done to help their children. Some have hired tutors and speech therapists or have paid for expensive programs that promise dramatic results. Others have moved to more remote locations, where lower costs of living would allow the mother to stop working and devote herself full-time to the care of her child. Other mothers have even broken up their marriages by divorcing a father who seemed not to understand or respond to the special needs of their special child.

Against this background of enormous caring and sacrifice, the actions and attitudes of too many "professionals" are especially appalling, as they hastily label and dogmatically treat children entrusted to their care. Superficial checklists, glib jargon and smug dismissals of parents as being "in denial" complete a picture of unbelievable pettiness and irresponsibility among too many people who describe themselves as being in the "helping" professions.

Sadly, such attitudes are not confined to those dealing with late-talking children. "Experts" of all sorts—whose money, careers, and egos depend on their presumed superiority to parents—have every incentive to apply their theories and dogmas to children, dismissing the first-hand experience of parents as mere laymen's illusions. Now that some of the children on whom they have made sweeping pronouncements have been followed for a few years—and will be followed all the way into adulthood by Professor Camarata—there will be a record for the first time of how often these "experts" have been wrong and by how wide a margin. Even at this early stage, it is already painfully apparent how hasty and reckless too many professionals and semi-professionals have been.

In the meantime, more respect for the dedication and first-hand knowledge of parents is very much in order and long overdue, whether in educational, therapeutic or other settings. Again, this is not just for parents of late-talking children, but for parents of children who encounter the growing armies of "experts" for all sorts of other reasons.

Parents need to know when to reject the guilt that too many others blithely lay on them, when to be skeptical towards fashionable labels and condescending attempts at intimidation, and when to stand up for their own child when what is being said and done makes no sense. Above all, parents need to understand that they are players, not pawns, and that they cannot let their child become a pawn in anyone else's game.

All of us need to understand that there are many incentives for "experts"—whether educators, therapists, or others—to denigrate parents in order to promote their own careers and agendas. While deficient parents exist, so do deficient people in many fields who want to take over parents' decisions, without taking over responsibility for the consequences.

We need to remember that it is parents who do not hesitate to stay up all night with a sick child or to sacrifice money, time, and career opportunities, in order to safeguard and promote the development of the young life that they have brought into this world. It is parents who have camped out all night when a good school opens up and takes applicants on a first-come-first-served basis. Parental dedication is an enormous capital asset that society cannot afford to waste because of passing fashions or simply because it is so taken for granted that it does not get the respect it deserves. Parents are a major asset, not only in terms of their dedication, but also in terms of their first-hand knowledge—knowledge that is too often waved aside by saying that parents are "in denial" when what they have seen with their own eyes does not match what the prevailing theories assume.

The kinds of children studied here can also be a major asset for society at large. In a norm-dominated and therapeutically oriented atmosphere, these children are all too often seen as bearers of "symptoms" and sources of "problems," when in fact their remarkable abilities represent golden opportunities. Attempts to adjust such children to norms and march them in lock-step with others can spoil and throw away gifts that few others possess, gifts that can make major contributions to society at large, as well as to the fulfillment of these children themselves.

NOTES

Chapter 1

1. D. V. M. Bishop and A. Edmundson, "Language-Impaired 4-Year-Olds: Distinguishing Transient from Persistent Impairment," *Journal of Speech and Hearing Disorders*, Vol. 52, No. 2 (May 1987), p. 166; Phil A. Silva, Rob McGee and Sheila M. Williams, "Developmental Language Delay from Three to Seven Years and Its Significance for Low Intelligence and Reading Difficulties at Age Seven," *Development Medicine and Child Neurology*, Vol. 25, No. 6 (December 1983), p. 783; Laurence B. Leonard, *Children with Specific Language Impairment* (Cambridge, Massachusetts: M.I.T. Press, 1998), p. 180.

2. Simon Baron-Cohen, et al. "Is There A Link Between Engineering and Autism?" *Autism*, 1997, pp. 105, 107.

3. See the specific listings by child in Thomas Sowell, *Late-Talking Children* (New York: Basic Books, 1997), pp. 88–92.

4. There is a reason for this age discrepancy. The last child to join my group did so in 1996, before the first child joined Professor Camarata's group in 1997. Moreover, the children in my group were surveyed either months or years after becoming part of the group, while the children who joined Stephen Camarata's group were surveyed at the time when they joined. Therefore it is not surprising that most of the children in my group were toilet trained by the time they were surveyed, while about half of the children in Camarata's group were not.

5. Joel N. Shurkin, *Terman's Kids: The Groundbreaking Study of How the Gifted Grow Up* (Boston: Little, Brown and Co., 1992), p. 46.

6. For reasons already explained in the note 4.

7. Margaret Morse Nice, "A Child Who Would Not Talk," *Pedagogical Seminary*, Vol. XXXII, No. 1 (March 1925), pp. 105, 130–134.

8. Joseph Adelson, "Seen but Not Heard," *Wall Street Journal*, August 25, 1997, p. A 16.

Chapter 2

1. Richard P. Feynmann, *"Surely You're Joking, Mr. Feynman": Adventures of a Curious Character* (New York: W. W. Norton & Co., 1985), p. 133.

2. *Ibid.*, pp. 119–120.

3. Kristine McKenna, "Mr. Feynman's Day Off," *Los Angeles Times*, November 27, 1994, Calendar Section, p. 7. His obituary described his lecture style in the classroom as an "impossible combination of theoretical physicist and circus barker, all body motion and sound effects." James Gleick, "Richard Feynman Dead at 69; Leading Theoretical Physicist," *New York Times*, February 17, 1999, p. A 1.

4. Christopher Sykes, *No Ordinary Genius: The Illustrated Richard Feynman* (New York: W. W. Norton, 1994), pp. 154–155.

5. Although Einstein was not part of the team of physicists working on the Manhattan Project, it was his letter to President Franklin D. Roosevelt that caused the project to be created in the first place and his contributions to physics that provided the principles used.

6. James Gleick, *Genius: The Life and Science of Richard Feynman* (New York: Pantheon Books, 1992), p. 25.

7. Denis Brian *Einstein: A Life* (New York: John Wiley & Sons, Inc., 1996), pp. 1–2.

8. Stanley A. Blumberg and Gwinn Owens, *Energy and Conflict: The Life and Times of Edward Teller* (New York: G. P. Putnam's Sons, 1976), p. 6.

9. Denis Brian, *Einstein*, p. 3.

10. Ronald W. Clark, *Einstein: The Life and Times* (New York: Wings Books, 1984), p. 13.

11. Roger Highfield and Paul Carter, *The Private Lives of Albert Einstein* (London: Faber and Faber, 1993), pp. 12–13.

12. Denis Brian, *Einstein*, p. 2.

13. John B. Severance, *Einstein: Visionary Scientist* (New York: Clarion Books, 1999), pp. 18–19.

14. Roger Highfield and Paul Carter, *The Private Lives of Albert Einstein*, pp. 11–12.

15. Peter Michelmore, *Einstein, Profile of a Man* (New York: Dodd, Mead, & Co. 1962), pp. 24, 31.

16. Stanley A. Blumberg and Gwinn Owens, *Energy and Conflict*, p. 6; Stanley A. Blumberg and Louis G. Panos, *Edward Teller: Giant of the Golden Age of Physics* (New York: Charles Scribner's Sons, 1990), pp. 15–16.

17. By and large, however, the children in Terman's study tended to be early in talking, though four boys and one girl from his group were two years old or older when they began talking and one boy in another group of high-IQ students began talking somewhere between age three and three and a half. See Lewis M. Terman, *Genetic Studies of Genius*, Volume I: *Mental and Physical Traits of a Thousand Gifted Children* (Stanford; Stanford University Press, 1925), pp. 186, 573; Lewis M. Terman and Melita H. Oden, *The Gifted Group at Mid-Life: Thirty-Five Years' Follow-Up of the Superior Child* (Stanford: Stanford University Press, 167), p. 7.

18. Constance Reid, *Julia: A Life in Mathematics* (The Mathematical Association of America, 1996), p. 5.

19. G. Gordon Liddy, *Will: The Autobiography of G. Gordon Liddy* (New York: St. Martin's Press, 1980), p. 1.

20. *Ibid.*, p. 52.

21. Stanley A. Blumberg and Gwinn Owens, *Energy and Conflict*, pp. 12, 21.

22. Constance Reid, *Julia*, p. 5.

23. H. J. Eysenck, Genius: The Natural History of Creativity (Cambridge: Cambridge University Press, 1995), p. 110

24. Stanley A. Blumberg and Gwinn Owens, *Energy and Conflict: The Life and Times of Edward Teller* (New York: G. P. Putnam's Sons, 1976), p. 16.

25. Berthold Litzmann, *Clara Schumann: An Artist's Life* (New York: Da Capo Press, 1979), p. 13.

26. Ibid., p. 4.

27. Nancy B. Reich, *Clara Schumann: The Artist and the Woman* (Ithaca: Cornell University Press, 1985), p. 32.

28. Betty Harding, *Concerto: The Story of Clara Schumann* (London: George G. Harrap & Co., Ltd.), pp. 10, 15.

29. Berthold Litzmann, *Clara Schumann*, pp. 1–2.

30. Nancy B. Reich, *Clara Schumann*, p. 37.

31. *Ibid.*, p. 25.

32. Harvey Sachs, *Rubinstein: A Life* (New York: Grove Press, 1995), p. 8.

33. Arthur Rubinstein, *My Young Years* (New York: Alfred A. Knopf, 1973), p. 4.

34. Harvey Sachs, *Rubinstein*, p. 8.

35. Harold C. Schonberg, "Arthur Rubinstein Dies in Geneva at 95," *New York Times*, December 21, 1982, p. A1.

36. Harvey Sachs, *Rubinstein*, p. 11.

37. *Ibid.*, p. 13.

38. Harold C. Schonberg, "Arthur Rubinstein Dies in Geneva at 95," *New York Times*, December 21, 1982, p. A1.

39. Harvey C. Schonberg, "Arthur Rubinstein Dies in Geneva at 95," *New York Times*, December 21, 1982, pp. A1 ff.

40. Thelma Weeks, *The Slow Speech Development of a Bright Child* (Lexington, Massachusetts: D. C. Heath and Co., 1974), p. 12.

41. *Ibid.*, pp. 10–12, 135, 143.

42. *Ibid.*, pp. 15–16.

43. *Ibid.*, p. 16.

44. *Ibid.*, p. 11.

45. *Ibid.*, p. 14.

46. *Ibid.*, pp. 22–23.

47. *Ibid.*, p. 136.

48. *Ibid.*, p. 34.

49. *Ibid.*, p. 35.

50. *Ibid.*, p. 15.

51. Marilyn Solomon, "Speechless at 3, Top Grad Has Final Word," *Nashua Telegraph*, June 25, 1994, p. 16.

52. "Only one in ten thousand to thirty thousand will score 160 or higher, and only one in a million will score above 180." Ellen Winner, Gifted Children: Myths and Realities (New York: Basic Books, 1996), p. 24

53. See, for example, Ellen Winner, Gifted Children (New York: Basic Books, 1996), pp. 246–248; Halbert B. Robinson, "A Case for Radical Acceleration: Programs of the Johns Hopkins University and the University of Washington," Academic Precocity: Aspects of Its Development, edited by Camilla Persson Benbow and Julian C. Stanley (Baltimore: Johns Hopkins University Press, 1983), p. 145; Camilla Persson Benbow and Julian C. Stanley, "Inequity in Equity: How 'Equity Can Lead to Inequity for High-

Potential Students," Psychology, Public Policy and Law, Vol. 2, No. 2 (June 1996), pp. 258–260; Donna L. Ernerson, "Summer Residential Programs: Academics and Beyond," Gifted Child Quarterly, Vol. 37, No. 4 (Fall 1993), pp. 171–172.

Chapter 3

1. Thelma E. Weeks, *The Slow Speech Development of a Bright Child*, p. 63.

2. Ellen Winner, *Gifted Children: Myths and Realities* (New York: Basic Books, 1996), p. 232.

3. *Ibid.*, p. 143.

4. Ibid, p. 24.

5. Laurence B. Leonard, *Children with Specific Language Impairment* (Cambridge, Massachusetts: M.I.T. Press, 2000), p. vii.

Chapter 4

1. Ellen Winner, *Gifted Children: Myths and Realities* (New York: Basic Books, 1996), pp. 160, 169; Norman Geschwind and Albert M. Galaburda, *Cerebral Lateralization: Biological Mechanisms, Associations, and Pathology* (Cambridge, Massachusetts: The MIT Press, 1987), pp. 15, 65–66, 99.

2. Miles G. Storfer, *Intelligence and Giftedness: The Contribution of Heredity and Early Environment* (San Francisco: Jossey-Bass, 1990), pp. 386, 389.

3. Camilla Persson Benbow, "Neuropsychological Perspectives on Mathematical Talent," *The Exceptional Brain: Neuropsychology of Talent and Special Abilities*, edited by Loraine K. Obler and Deborah Fein (New York: The Guilford Press, 1988), p. 58. See also Miles G. Storfer, *Intelligence and Giftedness: The Contribution of Heredity and Early Environment* (San Francisco: Jossey-Bass, 1990), p. 385.

4. Camilla Persson Benbow, op cit, p. 59; Miles D. Storfer, *Intelligence and Giftedness*, p. 384.

5. Ellen Winner, *Gifted Children*, p. 167.

6. Camilla Persson Benbow, "Possible Biological Correlates of Precocious Mathematical Reasoning Ability," *Trends in Neurosciences*, Vol. 10 (January 1987), p. 18. ; Lee D. Cranberg and Martin L. Albert, "The Chess Mind," *The*

Exceptional Brain: Neurophyschology of Talent and Special Abilities, edited by Loraine K. Obler and Deborah Fein (New York: The Guilford Press, 1988), p. 175.

7. Miles D. Storfer, *Intelligence and Giftedness*, pp. 384–385.

8. Diane F. Halpern, *Sex Differences in Cognitive Abilities* (Hillsdale, N.J.: Lawrence Erlbaum Associates, 1986), pp. 77–78. "Neurologists can temporarily paralyze one hemisphere by injecting sodium amytal into the carotid artery. A patient with a sleeping right hemisphere can talk; a patient with a sleeping left hemisphere cannot." Steven Pinker, *The Language Instinct* (New York: William Morrow, 1994), p. 300. "In about 98 % of the cases where brain damage leads to language problems, the damage is somewhere on the banks of the Sylvan fissure of the left hemisphere." *Ibid.*, p. 307.

9. Arnold B. Scheibel, "A Dendritic Correlate of Human Speech," *Cerebral Dominance: The Biological Foundations*, edited by Norman Geschwind and Albert M. Galaburda (Cambridge, Massachusetts: Harvard University Press, 1984), p. 43.

10. Thomas Ebert, et al., "Increased Cortical Representation of the Fingers of the Left Hand in String Players," *Science*, Vol. 270 (1981), pp. 305–307.

11. Brian Butterworth, *What Counts: How Every Brain is Hardwired for Math* (New York: The Free Press, 1999), p. 282.

12. Miles G. Storfer, *Intelligence and Giftedness*, pp. 390, 393.

13. Diane F. Halpern, *Sex Differences in Cognitive Abilities* (Hillsdale, N. J.: Lawrence Erlbaum Associates, 1986), p. 48.

14. Gina Kolata, "Men and Women Use Brain Differently, Study Discovers," *New York Times*, February 16, 1995, p. A 1; Bennet A. Shaywitze, et al, "Sex Differences in the Functional Organization of the Brain for Language," *Nature*, Vol. 373, No. 16 (February 1995), pp. 607–609; Deborah Blum, *Sex on the Brain: The Biological Differences Between Men and Women* (New York: Penguin Books, 1997), pp. 59, 61.

15. I happen to have encountered an example of such a person on a cruise ship in the Baltic—a very intelligent and highly analytical man who was also highly susceptible to irritants in the air. Although an American, he lived on the southwest coast of Ireland, where there were steady sea breezes and little in the air to aggravate his allergies. He took his vacations on cruise ships for the same reason, bringing with him duct tape with which to seal up the air-conditioning vents in his cabin, so that he could breathe only the fresh air off

the sea. An even more extreme example was Alan M. Turing, a British mathematical genius who was instrumental in breaking the supposedly unbreakable Enigma code used by the Germans in World War II. Turing suffered from allergies so badly that he sometimes wore a gas mask to filter out irritants in the air.

16. Miles D. Storfer, *Intelligence and Giftedness*, p. 385.

17. Camilla Persson Benbow, "Possible Biological Correlates of Precocious Mathematical Reasoning Ability," *Trends in Neurosciences*, Vol. 10 (January 1987), p. 18.

18. Marian Annett, *Left, Right, Hand and Brain: The Right Shift Theory* (London: Lawrence Erlbaum Associates, 1985), p. 118. See also Camilla Persson Benbow, op. cit., p. 58.

19. Steven Pinker, "His Brain Measured Up," *New York Times*, June 24, 1999, p. A11.

20. Dr. Sandra F. Witelson, who headed the team which examined Einstein's brain, said that one of its peculiarities was consistent with a well-known story that Einstein's mother was worried about his late development of speech. Lawrence K. Altman, "So This Is Why Einstein Was So Brilliant?" *New York Times*, June 18, 1999, p. A1. See also Steven Pinker, "His Brain Measured Up," *New York Times*, June 24, 1999, p. A27.

21. Steven Pinker, "His Brain Measured Up," *New York Times*, June 24, 1999, p. A11.

22. Steven Pinker, *The Language Instinct*, p. 289.

23. Margaret Morse Nice, "A Child Who Would Not Talk," *Pedagogical Seminary*, March 1925, Vol. XXXII, No. 1 (March 1925), p. 130.

24. Thelma E. Weeks, *The Slow Speech Development of a Bright Child* (Lexington, Massachusetts: D. C. Heath and Co., 1974), p. 37.

25. *Ibid.*, p. 136.

26. Ellen Winner, *Gifted Children*, pp. 163, 164, 344.

27. Deborah Fein and Loraine K. Obler, "Neuropsychological Study of Talent: A Developing Field," *The Exceptional Brain: Neuropsychology of Talent and Special Abilities*, edited by Lorain K. Obler and Deborah Fein (New York: Guilford Press, 1988), p. 6.

28. The two groups studied here are not the only ones for whom that is true. Similar results were found in research on children with "specific language impairment"—that is, children whose late-talking was not attributable to any visible physical or mental problem. Laurence B. Leonard, *Children with*

Specific Language Impairment (Cambridge, Massachusetts: MIT Press, 2000), p. 149.

29. "If the cause were in the environment—poor nutrition, hearing the defective speech of an impaired parent or sibling, watching too much TV, lead contamination from old pipes, whatever—then why would the syndrome capriciously strike some family members while leaving their near age-mates (in one case, a fraternal twin) alone? In fact, the geneticists working with Gopnik noted that the pedigree suggests a trait controlled by a single dominant gene, just like pink flowers on Gregor Mendel's pea plants." Steven Pinker, *The Language Instinct*, p. 49.

30. Philip S. Dale, et al., "Genetic Influence on Language in Two-Year-Old Children," *Nature Neuroscience*, Vol. 1, No. 4 (August 1998), p. 327.

31. Shannon Brownless, "Rare Disorder Reveals Split Between Language and Thought," *U. S. News & World Report*, June 15, 1998, p. 52.

32. Steven Pinker, *The Language Instinct*, p. 53.

33. "Williams Syndrome: Rare Disorder Reveals Split Between Language and Thought," *U.S. News & World Report*, June 16, 1998, pp. 51–52.

34. Michael Rossen, et al., "Interaction Between Language and Cognition: Evidence from Williams Syndrome," *Language, Learning, and Behavior Disorders*, edited by Joseph H. Beitchman, et al., p. 367.

35. "Williams Syndrome: Rare Disorder Reveals Split Between Language and Thought," *U.S. News & World Report*, June 16, 1998, pp. 51–52.

36. Oliver Sacks, *An Anthropologist on Mars* (New York: Vintage Books, 1995), p. 199.

37. *Ibid.*, p. 203. "Clearly, he recognizes that he is different, that he is special. He has a veritable passion for *Rain Man* and, one must suspect, identifies with the Dustin Hoffman character, perhaps the only autistic hero ever widely portrayed. He has the entire soundtrack of the film on tape and plays it continually on his Walkman. Indeed, he can recite large portions of the dialogue, taking every part, with perfect intonation." *Ibid.*, p. 231.

38. Ellen Winner, *Gifted Children*, p. 134.

39. Leon K. Miller, *Musical Savants: Exceptional Skill in the Mentally Retarded* (Hillsdale, N. J.: Lawrence Erlbaum Associates, 1989), p. 10. See also Thomas L Riis, "The Legacy of a Prodigy Lost in Mystery," *New York Times*, March 5, 2000, Arts & Leisure section, Part 2, p. 35.

40. Oliver Sacks, *An Anthropologist on Mars*, pp. 188–189.

41. Diane Armstrong, "Miracle on Parkgate Place," *The Australian Magazine*, April 14, 1989, p. 22.

42. Leon K. Miller, *Musical Savants: Exceptional Skills in the Mentally Retarded* (Hillsdale, N. J.: Lawrence Erlbaum Associates, Publishers, 1989), p. 203.

43. Bernard Rimland and Deborah Fein, "Special Talents of Autistic Savants," *The Exceptional Brain: Neurophyschology of Talent and Special Abilities*, edited by Loraine K. Obler and Deborah Fein (New York: The Guilford Press, 1988), pp. 487–488.

44. See, for example, Leon K. Miller, *Musical Savants*, pp. 2–3, 5–6, 19; Jean Bryant, *The Opening Door* (privately published in Australia), p. 67.

45. Leon K. Miller, *Musical Savants*, pp. 14, 15.

46. Bernard Rimland and Deborah Fein, "Special Talents of Autistic Savants," *The Exceptional Brain*, edited by Loraine K. Obler and Deborah Fein, p. 475.

47. Barnard Rimland and Deborah Fein, "Special Talents of Autistic Savants," *The Exceptional Brain*, edited by Loraine K. Obler and Deborah Fein, p. 488.

48. *Ibid.*

49. Michael Rossen, et al., "Interaction Between Language and Cognition: Evidence from Williams Syndrome," *Language, Learning, and Behavior Disorders: Developmental, Biological, and Clinical Perspectives*, edited by Joseph H. Beitchman, et al., (Cambridge: Cambridge University Press, 1996), p. 376.

50. Steven Pinker, *The Language Instinct*, p. 289.

51. *Ibid.*, pp. 293–296.

52. *Ibid.*, p. 293.

53. Susan Martins Miller, *Reading Too Soon: How to Understand and Help the Hyperlexic Child* (Elmhurst, Illinois: Center for Speech and Language Disorders, 1993), p. 13.

54. *Ibid.*, p. 5.

55. Digby Tantam, "Asperger Syndrome in Adulthood," *Autism and Asperger Syndrome* (Cambridge: Cambridge University Press, 1991), pp. 147–183; Francesca E. Happé, "The Autobiographical Writings of Three Asperger Syndrome Adults: Problems of Interpretation and Implications for Theory," *Ibid.*, pp. 207–242.

56. Ellen Winner, *Gifted Children*, pp. 225–226.

57. The standard reference book for psychologists and psychiatrists, *The Diagnostic and Statistical Manual*, says the same.

58. Simon Baron-Cohen, et al., "Is There a Link Between Engineering and Autism?" *Autism*, 1997, No. 1, pp. 105, 106, 107.

59. Susan Martins Miller, *Reading Too Soon: How to Understand and Help the Hyperlexic Child* (Elmhurst, Illinois: Center for Speech and Language Disorders, 1993), p. 14.

60. Ellen Winner, *Gifted Children*, pp. 133, 223–225, 357 (note 22).

Chapter 5

1. Patricia McAleer Hamaguchi, *Childhood Speech, Language, and Listening Problems: What Every Parent Should Know* (New York: John Wiley & Sons, Inc. 1995) p. 90.

2. Ellen Winner, *Gifted Children: Myths and Realities* (New York: Basic Books, 1996), p. 329, note 15.

3. A personal experience of mine may illustrate the point. As a beginning student in economics, I was the only person in my tutorial group who found the lesson on Say's Law incomprehensible. I was able to understand the concept only years later, when writing a doctoral dissertation on the subject. This dissertation was subsequently enlarged into a book titled *Say's Law*, which was praised in scholarly journals in the United States and overseas. But Say's Law made no sense to me when taught at the superficial level used for beginning students.

4. Thelma E. Weeks, *The Slow Speech Development of a Bright Child*, p. 63.

5. See, for example, Lynn H. Fox, et al., editors, *Learning-Disabled/Gifted Children: Identification and Programming* (Baltimore: University Park Press, 1983); Candice Feiring and Lawrence T. Taft, "The Gifted Learning Disabled Child: Not a Paradox," *Pediatric Annals*, Vol. 14, No. 10 (1985), pp. 729–732; Susan Baum, "Meeting the Needs of Learning Disabled Gifted Children," *Roeper Review*, Vol. 7, No. 1 (1984), pp. 16–19.

6. Candice Feiring and Lawrence T. Taft, "The Gifted Learning Disabled Child: Not a Paradox," *Pediatric Annals*, Vol. 14, No. 10 (1985), p. 729.

7. Abraham J. Tannenbaum and Lois J. Baldwin, "Giftedness and Learning Disability: A Paradoxical Combination," *Learning-Disabled/Gifted Children*, edited by Lynn H. Fox, et al., editors, pp. 21, 28.

8. Abraham J. Tannenbaum and Lois J. Baldwin, "Giftedness and Learning Disability: A Paradoxical Combination," *Learning-Disabled/Gifted Children*, edited by Lynn H. Fox , et al. (Baltimore: University Park Press, 1983), p. 22.

9. Bernard Rimland, "Plain Talk about PDD and the Diagnosis of Autism," *Autism Research Review International*, Vol. 7, No. 2 (1993).

10. Bernard Rimland, "Foreword," Temple Grandin and Margaret M. Scarino, *Emergence Labeled Autistic* (Novato, California: Arena Press, 1986), p. 5.

11. See, for example, Martin L. Gross, *The Conspiracy of Ignorance: The Failure of American Public Schools* (New York: HarperCollins, 1999), pp. 43–45; Garaldine Jonçich Clifford and James W. Guthrie, *Ed School: A Brief for Professional Education* (Chicago: University of Chicago Press, 1988), p. 141; Sue Berryman, *Who Will Do Science?* (New York: The Rockefeller Foundation, 1983), pp. 74–75; W. Timothy Waver, *America's Teacher Quality Problem: Alternatives for Reform* (New York: Praeger Publishers, 1983), pp. 39–58, 163–173; Ernest Boyer, *High School: A Report on Secondary Education in America* (New York: Harper & Row, 1983), pp. 171–172; William H. Whyte, *The Organization Man* (New York: Simon & Schuster, 1956), p. 83.

12. Patricia McAleer Hamaguchi, *Childhood Speech, Language & Listening Problems: What Every Parent Should Know* (New York: John Wiley & Sons, 1995), p. 96.

13. Laurence B. Leonard, *Children with Specific Language Development* (Cambridge, Massachusetts: M.I.T. Press, 1998), p. 180.

14. See, for example, Herb Kutchins and Stuart A. Kirk, *Making Us Crazy: DSM: The Psychiatric Bible and the Creation of Mental Disorders* (New York: The Free Press, 1997).

Chapter 6

1. D. V. M Bishop and A. Edmundson, "Language-Impaired 4-Year-Olds: Distinguishing Transient from Persistent Impairment," *Journal of Speech and Hearing Disorders*, Vol. 52, No. 2 (May 1987), pp. 156–173.

2. Patricia MacAleer Hamaguchi, *Childhood Speech, Language and Listening Problems*, p. 20.

3. "Speaking Out on Speech Therapy," *Family Life*, July/August 1997, pp. 18–19.

4. Even *Time* magazine listed characteristics of Bill Gates that paralleled those of people with autism. "Diagnosing Bill Gates," *Time*, January 24, 1994, p. 25.

5. D. V. M. Bishop and A. Edmundson, "Language-Impaired 4-Year-Olds: Distinguishing Transient from Persistent Impairment," *Journal of Speech and Hearing Disorders*, Vol. 52, No. 2 (May 1987), p. 166.

6. Phil A. Silva, Rob McGee and Sheila M. Williams, "Developmental Language Delay from Three to Seven Years and Its Significance for Low Intelligence and Reading Difficulties at Age Seven," *Development Medicine and Child Neurology*, Vol. 25, No. 6 (December 1983), p. 783.

7. Margaret Morse Nice, "A Child Who Would Not Talk," *Pedagogical Seminary*, Vol. XXXII, No. 1 (March 1925), p. 133

Chapter 7

1. Halbert B. Robinson, "A Case for Radical Acceleration: Programs of the Johns Hopkins University and the University of Washington," *Academic Precocity: Aspects of Its Development*, edited by Camilla Persson Benbow and Julian C. Stanley (Baltimore: Johns Hopkins University, 1983), p. 145.

2. Julian C. Stanley, "Rationale of the Study of Mathematically Precocious Youth (SMPY) During Its First Five Years of Promoting Educational Acceleration," *The Gifted and the Creative: A Fifty-Year Perspective*, edited by Julian C. Stanley, et al. (Baltimore: Johns Hopkins University Press, 1977), p. 85.

3. Leta S. Hollingsworth, *Children Above 180 IQ: Origin and Development* (Yonkers, N.Y.: World Book Co., 1942), pp. 260–263, 278, *passim.*

4. Ellen Winner, *Gifted Children*, pp. 227–229; Ann Berghout Austin and Dianne C. Draper, "Peer Relationships of the Academically Gifted," *Gifted Child Quarterly*, Vol. 25, No. 3 (Summer 1981), pp. 131–132.

5. Diane F. Halpern, *Sex Differences in Cognitive Abilities* (Hillsdale, N. J.: Lawrence Erlbaum Associates, 1986), p. 46.

6. Leta S. Hollingsworth, *Children Above 180 IQ*, pp. 300–302.

7. *Ibid.*, pp. 270.

8. *Ibid.*, p. 287

9. David Lubinski and Camilla Persson Benbow, "States of Excellence," *American Psychologist*, Vol. 55, No. 1 (January 2000), p. 139.

10. Ellen Winner, *Gifted Children*, p. 226.

11. Lynn Daggett Pollins, "The Effects of Acceleration on The Social and Emotional Development of Gifted Students," *Academic Precocity: Aspects of Its Development* (Baltimore: Johns Hopkins University Press, 1983), pp. 160–178.

12. Halbert B. Robinson, "A Case for Radical Acceleration: Programs of the Johns Hopkins University and the University of Washington," *Academic Precocity: Aspects of Its Development*, edited by Camilla Persson Benbow (Baltimore: Johns Hopkins University, 1983), p. 142.

13. Donald L. Enersen, "Summer Residential Programs: Academics and Beyond," *Gifted Child Quarterly*, Vol. 37, No. 4 (Fall 1993), pp. 169–176.

14. *Ibid.*, p. 145.

15. A fourth-grader who was able to score higher than the average high school senior on the mathematics portion of the Scholastic Aptitude Test was nevertheless taught the same math as his classmates on grounds that it would be "a violation of social justice" to teach him a higher level of mathematics. Camilla Persson Benbow and Julian C. Stanley, "Inequity in Equity: How 'Equity' Can Lead to Inequity for High-Potential Students," *Psychology, Public Policy & Law*, Vol. 2. No. 2 (June 1996), p. 272. See also, Donna Enerson, "Summer Residential Programs: Academics and Beyond," *Gifted Child Quarterly*, Vol. 37, No. 4 (Fall 1993), p. 171.

Epilogue

1. Margaret Morse Nice, "A Child Who Would Not Talk," *Pedagogical Seminary*, Vol. XXXII, No. 1 (March 1925), pp. 105-142

2. "ASHA Responds to Sowell's Column on Late Talkers," *ASHA Leader*, December 21, 1999, p. 3.

3. The only reasonable basis for the critic's confusion is that, in order to save space and not burden those who were filling out the questionnaire, I presented a list of analytical occupations for parents to check as regards other close relatives. But the parents themselves had a blank to fill in as they wished for their own occupations.

4. Philip S. Dale, et al., "Genetic Influence on Language Delay in Two-Year-Old Children," *Nature Neuroscience*, Vol. 1, No. 4 (August 1998), pp. 324–328. A summary of this research can be found in "Speaking of Twins," *Ibid.*, pp. 259–260.

5. Like some other brain functions which malfunction more often among people with high analytical ability, portions of the brain associated with music are "all within the left hemisphere." N. Wertheim, "Is There an Anatomical Localisation for Musical Faculties," *Music and the Brain: Studies in the*

Neurology of Music, edited by MacDonald Critchley (London: William Heinemann Medical Books, Ltd., 1977), p. 289.

APPENDIX

Rather than have the first chapter of this book look like a Census publication laden with numbers, I have saved some of the tables for presentation here, for those researchers who want more details, or who want to know more about the samples and their presentation. However, even this Appendix does not contain tabulations of all the answers to all the questions in the questionnaires filled out by parents of late-talking children. Those who want the complete computerized tabulations can obtain them by writing to me at The Hoover Institution, Stanford University, Stanford, California 94305.

Part I of this Appendix gives the numbers and Part II discusses the methods.

Part I: Statistical Data

The most basic data are those on the size of the samples in the two studies and the internal breakdown of this sample. This is given in Table 1 below.

Table 1: SAMPLE SIZE

	ORIGINAL STUDY	CAMARATA STUDY
TOTAL NUMBER OF CHILDREN	46	239
male	39	202
female	7	37
TOTAL NUMBER OF FAMILIES	44	235
NUMBER OF BIOLOGICAL FAMILIES	43	232
NUMBER OF BIOLOGICAL CHILDREN	45	236
male	38	200
female	7	36

TABLE 2A: AGE OF BEGINNING TO TALK (ORIGINAL GROUP)

	before 1	1 to 1½	1½ to 2	2 to 2½	2½ to 3	3 to 3½	3½ to 4	4 to 4½	4½ to 5	5 +	not yet
FIRST WORD	5	8	5	9	6	5	2	2	0	1	1
FIRST MULTI-WORD STATEMENT	0	1	3	3	6	4	7	9	2	3	5
FIRST SENTENCE	0	0	0	0	1	5	5	9	7	10	7
CONVERSATION	0	0	0	0	0	2	7	10	4	14	7

TABLE 2B: AGE OF BEGINNING TO TALK (CAMARATA GROUP)

	before 1	1 to 1½	1½ to 2	2 to 2½	2½ to 3	3 to 3½	3½ to 4	4 to 4½	4½ to 5	5 +	not yet	no data
FIRST WORD	50	71	33	35	23	6	5	1	1	*	4	8
FIRST MULTI-WORD STATEMENT	1	9	19	37	39	34	12	13	1	1	61	11
FIRST SENTENCE	*	*	3	7	13	29	23	19	5	6	121	12
CONVERSATION	*	*	*	2	6	19	18	19	13	11	138	12

* no data collected in these categories, presumably because no one was expected to be in these categories

Data for biological families and biological children are listed separately for use in analysis involving possible hereditary traits. My sample and Professor Camarata's sample are mutually exclusive. Membership in my group was closed before his group began to be formed and he did not accept any members of my group into his group, even though some members of my group sought and received his professional advice regarding their children. The data presented here for his group is for that group as it existed on June 1, 2000, even though it has continued to grow since then.

As noted in Chapter 1, the difference between the total number of children and the number of biological children in my original study is due to one child who was adopted. In Professor Camarata's study, the difference is due to two children who were adopted and one whose father was an unknown sperm donor. One of the mothers was also adopted, so all of her children's biological grandparents are not known, but she and they are still counted as part of the sample of biological families. However, the occupations of the children's uncles and aunts—which include three pilots—were not counted in our occupational tables because there is no way to know whether these uncles and aunts were their father's siblings or their mother's siblings—and, if the latter, whether they were siblings in the mother's biological or adopted family. Nor were the occupations of their maternal grandparents counted for the same reason. Efforts to contact the parents for clarification were unsuccessful, since they were no longer at the same address as when they filled out their questionnaire.

When did all these children begin to talk and when did their parents begin to worry? As noted in Chapter 1, much depends on whether "talking" is defined as saying a word, making multi-word statements, speaking in complete sentences, or engaging in back-and-forth conversation. Table 2A (shown at left) gives the data for my original sample and Table 2B (shown at left) gives the data for Professor Camarata's sample:

By any reasonable criterion, the children in both groups are very late in beginning to speak. when did their parents become seriously concerned about that fact? Obviously it varied and the variations are shown on Table 3.

TABLE 3: AGE AT WHICH PARENT BECAME SERIOUSLY CONCERNED

	BEFORE AGE 1	1 TO 1 ½ YEARS	1 ½ TO 2 YEARS	2 TO 2 ½ YEARS	2 ½ TO 3 YEARS	3 YEARS +
ORIGINAL STUDY	0	4	2	17	12	11
CAMARATA STUDY	2	9	42	91	57	37

What specific reasons caused these parents to be concerned? the various reasons are shown in Table 4.

TABLE 4: PRIMARY REASON FOR PARENTS CONCERN

	CHILD'S FRUSTRATION	DAILY PROBLEMS	BEHIND SCHEDULE	OTHER
ORIGINAL STUDY	4	1	31	10
CAMARATA STUDY	27	22	156	34

The incidence of musicians among the close relatives of the children in the two studies is shown in Table 5.

TABLE 5: MUSICIANS AMONG THE CHILD'S RELATIVES

	AT LEAST ONE CLOSE RELATIVE WHO PLAYS MUSIC	MULTIPLE MUSICIANS	PROFESSIONAL MUSICIANS
ORIGINAL STUDY (45)	35	26	12
CAMARATA STUDY (223)	185	156	67

When relatives who are either in highly analytical occupations or who play a musical instrument are considered together, the great majority of the children in both groups had both among their close relatives, an average of 4 per child. See Table 6 below.

TABLE 6: CLOSE RELATIVES IN ANALYTICAL OCCUPATIONS OR MUSICIANS

	AT LEAST ONE	TWO OR MORE	THREE OR MORE
ORIGINAL STUDY (45 BIOLOGICAL CHILDREN)	44	39	32
CAMARATA STUDY (223 BIOLOGICAL CHILDREN)	224	215	195

The fact that families differ in size and composition makes it hard to achieve the strict comparability that we would like, in order to know just how unusual the families studied are, compared to families in the general population. One way of achieving at least one kind of standardization would be to look at just parents and grandparents. Although families differ in the number of uncles, aunts, and siblings they contain, they all have two biological parents and four biological grandparents. We could look at how many of these six people are in various analytical occupations and how many play musical instruments. However, that would produce more tables than necessary, even for an Appendix. It may be useful as an illustration to select just one prominent occupation—engineers. Since few of these children's female relatives are engineers, Table 7 shows the percentage of fathers and grandfathers who are engineers.

TABLE 7: FATHERS AND GRANDFATHERS WHO ARE ENGINEERS

BIOLOGICAL CHILDREN	FATHERS	GRANDFATHERS
ORIGINAL STUDY: (45 CHILDREN)	20%	33%
CAMARATA STUDY (236 CHILDREN)	22%	38%

Those who wish to determine the frequency of other occupations among the parents and grandparents can obtain the raw data from me at the address already mentioned.

Since there are twice as many grandfathers as fathers, it is not surprising that there are more engineers among the grandfathers. One of the other characteristics of the children in both studies is lateness in becoming toilet trained. There is considerable variation among them, as shown in Table 8 (page 198).

TABLE 8: AGE OF TOILET TRAINING

AGE	URINATION (ORIGINAL STUDY)	URINATION (CAMARATA STUDY)	BOWEL MOVEMENT (ORIGINAL STUDY)	BOWEL MOVEMENT (CAMARATA STUDY)
BEFORE 1	0	*	0	*
1 TO 1 ½	0	1	0	4
1 ½ TO 2	2	0	2	0
2 TO 2 ½	2	10	1	4
2 ½ TO 3	4	13	3	6
3 TO 3 ½	13	35	9	26
3 ½ TO 4	6	22	8	14
4 TO 4 ½	5	16	5	21
4 ½ TO 5	5	4	4	5
5+	4	2	8	2
NOT YET	3	120	4	138
NO DATA	2	16	2	19

* no data collected in this category, presumably because it was assumed that no one would be in this category.

The physical skills of the children in both studies:

TABLE 9: PHYSICAL SKILLS OF ALL CHILDREN

BIOLOGICAL CHILDREN	ABOVE AVERAGE	AVERAGE	CLUMSY
ORIGINAL STUDY	26 percent	39 percent	35 percent
CAMARATA STUDY	37 percent	42 percent	21 percent

Part II: Methods

The two main kinds of statistical complications in the tables shown in Chapter 1 are those involving (1) trying to maintain comparability between my original data and the data from Professor Camarata's study, and (2) complications inherent in my original tabulations themselves.

Reconciling Differences between the Studies

Fortunately, the forms used by Stephen Camarata were very similar to those used in my study, so in most cases there were no important differences in the terms and methods used. However, it is worth clarifying what differences do exist.

In the table on puzzle skills, for example, my data were broken down into four categories: Unusually Good, Average, Below Average, and Not Noticed. Camarata's categories are identical for the first three but he then has both Unknown and Omitted. In the table in Chapter 1, his Unknown category is taken as meaning essentially what my Not Noticed category meant. The Omitted data were then simply subtracted from his Grand Total and the percentages then refer to percentages among those parents who answered at all. Fortunately, only 3 out of 128 parents omitted a response, so the percentages were affected very little. Moreover, anyone who prefers another way of handling this can add the three back to see what difference it makes.

Similarly, in the table on memory, there is an Omitted category in Professor Camarata's data, but not in mine. Here the parents of two children omitted a response and, following the same procedure again, I simply subtracted those two from his Grand Total before computing percentages. There were also two omissions subtracted from the totals used to calculate the percentages of children falling into various categories in the table on social interactions. There was only one omission in the table showing why parents considered their child's late talking to be a problem. Professor Camarata has a finer breakdown in his data, listing which reason appeared alone, which appeared in combination with other reasons, and the respective orders of the reasons each time. My table simply condenses all that— with, of course, the various categories adding up to more than 100 percent in both studies.

In *Late-Talking Children*, the occupations of close relatives and the close relatives playing musical instruments were presented as simple absolute numbers. However, because the sample sizes differ so much between my study and that of Professor Camarata, the tables in the first chapter of this book are presented as percentages, in order to facilitate comparisons between the two sets of data. This in turn raises the question of which families are to be counted in figuring these percentages. Since we are discussing possible hereditary influences, clearly only biological families should be counted. Fortunately, for this purpose, there is only one adopted child in my original group, so that 43 of the 44 families are biological. However, this small difference is enough to create small differences between some of the percentages cited in the text of *Late-Talking Children* and those cited in the tables in this book. The absolute numbers nevertheless remain the same.

Among the data not tabulated in this book are those on the number of children diagnosed at some point or other as autistic. This is because a number of such diagnoses were contradicted by other diagnoses of the same child or by the later history of the child. The latter applies especially in my grooup, where the children have been followed for more years than the children in Camarata's group. In my survey, "pervasive developmental disorder" was equated with autism, but *not* in Professor Camarata's study.

In some of the tables showing the ages at which various children first spoke or were first toilet trained there are some cells with an asterisk in them to indicate that no such category appeared in Professor Camarata's study. For example, he had no category for children who spoke their first word at age five or older, since he expected no such children to be in the sample. My sample included all the categories from "before age one" to "5+". Incidentally, in making the age breakdowns, from "1 to 1 1/2" includes children 12 months old up to–but not including–children 18 months old. similarly for the other age breakdowns.

The First Study

In order to facilitate interpretation of the data from the 1996 questionnaire, I include the instructions used for making those tabulations. as well as a copy of the original questionnaire.

I. EARLY CHILDHOOD

1. At what age did you become seriously concerned because your child was not talking? _____

2. Why was the child's late talking considered to be a problem *at that time*? (Check box below. If more than one reason, put a 1 in the box of the most important reason, 2 in the box for the next most important, etc.)

   The child was unhappy at not being able
   to communicate. ☐

   Parents were unhappy with the day to day
   problems caused by the child's not talking. ☐

   The normal time for the child to talk had
   come and gone, causing concern for
   the child's future. ☐

   Other (write below and/or on back of pages: _____
   _____

3. Check which of the following apply to your child:

Left-handed	Right-handed	Ambidextrous
☐	☐	☐
Many or severe allergies	Few or mild allergies	Practically no allergies
☐	☐	☐
Many or severe ear infections	Few or mild ear infections	Practically no ear infections
☐	☐	☐
Clumsy for his or her age	Average in physical skills	Above average in physical skills
☐	☐	☐
Unusually good at puzzles, such as putting cut-out shapes into a board	About average at such things for children the same age	Below average at such puzzles
☐	☐	☐

Ability at such puzzles never tested or noticed
☐

Child fascinated by:

water (in tubs or streams, pools, lakes, etc.)	spinning objects	Other
☐	☐	☐

If "other," please specify: _____

_____

_____

No special fascinations: ☐

4. Did the child in early childhood prefer toys aimed at girls, such as dolls, or toys aimed at boys, such as toy trucks or trains, or was ther no difference in his or her preferences?

Generally preferred toys for girls	Generally preverred toys for boys	No preference
☐	☐	☐

5. Were playmates of one sex preferred to the other in setting where both were available?

Preferred to play with girls   ☐

Preferred to play with boys   ☐

No particular preference either way   ☐

Only boys usually available   ☐

Only girls usually available   ☐

II. FAMILY BACKGROUND

1. Child's place in the family:

Only child	First born	Youngest	Adopted
☐	☐	☐	☐

Others (please specify): _____

Number of sisters: _____

Number of brothers: _____

Is there a sibling or other close relative who talked late? ____

Are there significantly more boys than girls, or vice versa, among our relatives? _____

2. Family educational and occupational backgrounds:

Parent's education:
Level_____ (diploma or degree)
Specialization _____ (field)

Parents' Occupations
Mother: _____
Father: _____

Family occupational backgrounds:

(please put a number in each cell to indicate how many family members in each category have worked in the occupation in question)

	Father	Mother	Grandfathers	Grandmothers	Aunts	Uncles
Accountants						
Computer Specialists						
Engineers						
Mathematicians						
Physicians						
Pilots						
Scientists						
Other analytical (please specify)						

Please write an **M** in the appropriate box for each relative who plays or has played a musical instrument. Put an asterisk alongside the **M** for each ne who played professionally or taught music.

3. Ethnic background: MOTHER   FATHER

European or White   ☐   ☐

African or Black   ☐   ☐

Chinese or Japanese   ☐   ☐

American Indian or   ☐   ☐
    Native american

India Indian   ☐   ☐

Other (please specify):   ☐   ☐

III. TALKING

1. Age when the child's first work was spoke _____

2. Age when the child's first statement was made using more than
    one word   _____

3. Age when the child first spoke in complete sentences _____

4. Age when back-and-forth conversation first occurred _____

5. To what extent has the child's talking been accompanied by
    gestures, facial expressions, and/or body language coordinated-
    with the words? Indicate by checking a box in the table below:

Much more so than most children the same age	
Somewhat more so than most children the same age	
Average for children the same age	
Somewhat less than average for the age	
Much less than average for the age	

IV. SOCIAL DEVELOPMENT

How would you characterize the child's ability to handle social relations?

FAR BELOW AVERAGE ☐

BELOW AVERAGE ☐

AVERAGE ☐

ABOVE AVERAGE ☐

FAR ABOVE AVERAGE ☐

V. MENTAL ABILITY

1. Indicate on the table below the age or ages at which you child's mental ability was tested, the name of the test, and the test scores or other index of his ability that resulted.

AGES	NAME OF TEST	SCORE OR OTHER INDICATOR
AGE:		
AGE:		
AGE:		
AGE:		

2. Please check one of the boxes below to indicate how you would characterize the child's memory.

Very poor	Below average	Average	Above average	Extremely good
☐	☐	☐	☐	☐

VI. MISCELLANEOUS

1. Evaluations

Have medical or psychological specialists examined your child as a result of his or her late talking?

	YES		NO
	☐		☐

Please indicate at what age these examinations took place, the profession of the person doing the examination (physician, psychologist, etc.), the process, and the results on the table below:

EXAMINATION		TITLES OF PERSONS EXAMINING THE CHILD	NAME OF TEST OR PROCEDURE	WAS THE PROCESS ITSELF STRESSFUL TO THE CHILD	WHAT CONCLUSION WAS REACHED AFTER EXAMINATION
CHILD'S AGE ON THE FIRST OCCASION					
CHILD'S AGE ON THE SECOND OCCASION					
CHILD'S AGE ON THE THIRD OCCASION					
CHILD'S AGE ON THE FOURTH OCCASION					

2. Child's Likes and Dislikes

Things especially liked by the child: _____

Things especially disliked by the child: _____

3. Have you had a speech therapist work with your child?

           YES   NO

           ☐   ☐

At what ages? _____

With what results? _____

4. At what age did the child become toilet-trained?

For urination: _____

For bowel movements:_____

VII. GROUP ACTIVITY

Please check whichever statements below apply to you:

I have written letters to the group as a whole.   ☐

I have written individual members of the group   ☐
without writing the group as a whole.

I have phone other member(s) of the group.   ☐

I have been phoned by other member(s) of the group.   ☐

I have met other member(s) in person.   ☐

I always read letters and memos from the group.   ☐

I usually read letters and memos from the group.   ☐

I seldom read letters and memos from the group.   ☐

I never read letters and memos.   ☐

PLEASE ADD ANY ADDITIONAL INFORMATION, EITHER
FOR ITS OWN SAKE OR TO CLARIFY ANSWERS ALREADY
GIVEN:

Information in this and previus questionnaire may be shown to physicians or other professionals doing research on this group, with our permission, as indicated by signing below. Family names will not be used in any publication nor will small communities be identified. If there are any other restrictions you wish, please indicate them before signing below:

NAME (printed)   _____

SIGNATURE: _____

ADDRESS: _____

_____

_____

_____

TELEPHONE NUMBER: _____

Question:	**Clarification:**
Male / Female Categories	This refers to the number of male and female <u>individuals</u>, not the number of families with two late-talking children each, the number of individuals and the number of families will of course not coincide . More important, for most questions, the relevant answer is in terms of individuals but for other it is families.
Section I, Question 1	Since the age categories overlap, "1 to 1 ½ years" will mean <u>between</u> age one and age one and a half, so that a child who was exactly one and a half years old when his parents became concerned about his not talking, would be recorded in the category "1 ½ to 2 years." The same principal applies to all age categories. Because this is a question about <u>parents</u>, we do not wish to count the same parents twice where there is more than one late-talking child in the family, so the number that is relevant here is the number of families, not individuals.
Section I, Question 2	Since this is also a question about parents, again, the number here refers to the number of families, not individuals.
Section I, Question 3	Since this is a question about children the number here refers to individuals—as do all other numbers not specifically referring to families.
Section II, Question 1	This number should refer to families. Otherwise, not only will twins who talk late automatically count as two individuals with a relative who talked late, but each of their relatives who talked late will also be counted twice.
Section II, Question 2 "Occupations" Table	The "occupations" tables is a family table. That is, if two-late talking children in the same family have an uncle who is an accountant, that does not mean two accountants. This is a family table in another and more fundamental sense: What we ultimately want to know is what percentage of the families have an engineer, an accountant, etc., among the late-talking children's close relatives. That means that two uncles in one family who are accountants count as one accountant for this table.

(continues)

Question:	Clarification:
Section II, Question 2 (continued)	Otherwise, if only one out of three families had an accountant among the children's close relatives, while that one family had three accountants, when only 33% did. Therefore, no matter how many relatives might be listed on the questionnaires as being in a given occupation, enter just one for that occupation in that family. In this table, we are not counting the number of relatives who are accountants; we are counting the number where there is at least one relative who works in that occupation.
Section II, Question 1 "more boys than girls or vice-versa"	If there is not a sex imbalance on <u>both</u> sides of the family, this should be recorded as "no great difference". Where the question does not indicate whether it applies to the mother or father's relatives, then assume to both and enter it accordingly.
Section II, Question 2	This is also a family table showing the number of families that have musicians among the close relatives of the late-talking children. If there is more than one musician, that does not change the number in the "yes" column but such families will also be counted (as one) in the "multiple" column. In other words, the same family can be counted in more than one column here.
Section II, Question 3	This is a family question, so that parents are not counted more than once when they have more than one child who talks late.
Section III, IV, V and VI	All these are to be entered as individuals.
Section V "Intelligence Quotient"	Where there are multiple scores, count the highest.
Section VI, Question1	Count "pervasive development disorder" (PDD) as autism.
Section VII	This is to be entered by family, to avoid counting the parents of multiple late-talkers more than once.

INDEX